Sonya, from one praying k
I feel you deeply. Alki
Always in my prayers.

Sabrina
11. 13. 2018

PICK UP THE PHONE LORD! IT'S AN EMERGENCY!

THE red phone CHRONICLES

PICK UP THE PHONE LORD! IT'S AN EMERGENCY!

WRITTEN BY

SABRINA HAYES

DESIGN & LAYOUT BY CHRISTOPHER HAYES

This book is dedicated to my family during the year 2017.

To my husband Christopher, and my "baby" girls, Victoria, Jordan, and Cameron.

We experienced so much in 2017, and I got all of it on paper. We had so many hopes, both realized and crushed, so much to feel, so much to cry over, but yet so much to celebrate, so many new dreams, and so much to be thankful for.

And Our Lord had a Word for us concerning all of it. At every turn He spoke.

This is our book guys.

This book is also dedicated to my Bigmama.

She told me years ago that thousands of people would hear God's Word through my voice. And that they would actually listen.

I told her she was crazy.

I hope she sees me from Heaven.

You were right, Bigmama.

You were right.

•THE
directory

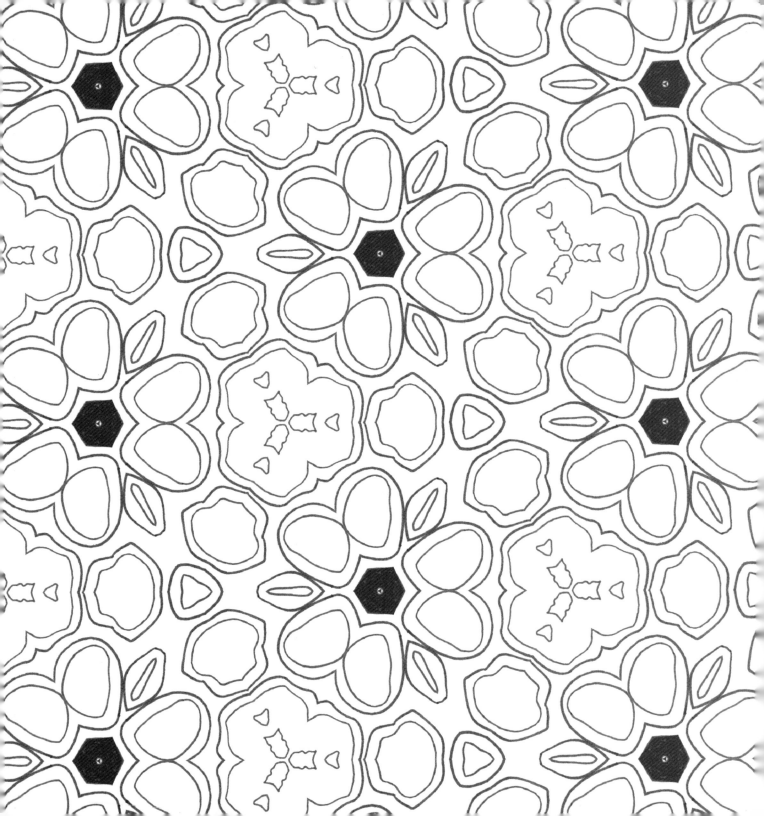

introduction

I journal a lot.

Like a WHOLE lot.

I have a leather chest filled with journals from past seasons that sits on my office bookshelf like a collection of stories from my past just waiting to be included in a faith time capsule of sorts. My journals are essentially my problems, my praises, my people, and my most intimate of conversations all written down, but with God's responses included.

God's responses? What do you mean God's responses?

Call it eerie. Call it weird. Call it slightly looney-binnish if you'd like, but He speaks back to me. All the time. Whether it be through a devotional, directly from Scripture, a post I "just happened" upon on social media, or a quick text from an otherwise-clueless-about-what-I'm-feeling friend… He responds to me. It happens all the time. So I capture it in words so that I don't miss what He's saying. It's pretty incredible to see on paper.

Fast forward to this last journal…2017; or half of it anyway. A tremendous year of personal, professional, family, and faith change, growth, and trial:

I quit my job in direct sales to become a full-time Women's Minister.
I took a (GIANT) leap off of a risk cliff and introduced the world to a Faith Planner I created.
My husband had a brain aneurysm.
I moved two kids out of the house.
I poured my heart into the conception and launch of a nationwide Women's Ministry.
And some other, more personal, stuff I'm pretty sure my husband would kill me over if I wrote it here.

Needless to say, 2017 was a tumultuous year.

Tears. Fears. Changing careers. You name it, we felt it.

And I got all of it on paper, in this shiny pink and gold journal with pineapples on it.

I sought after God's voice, His promise, and His help with every fiber of my being. There were times when I was so desperate for His reply to my pleas that I thought I would die if He didn't respond to Me. But He always did. Always.

It got to the point where I couldn't wait to meet Him every morning. I would write my initial thoughts on paper and then dive into my devotional and Scriptures because I KNEW He would respond.

And He always did.

Always.

And I captured all of it. On paper. In the pages between two pink covers with pineapples on them.

If I said I'm sad, He asked why.
If I said I'm scared, He said I didn't create you that way.
If I said I'm tired of waiting, He said wait more.
If I said I'm anxious, He said give it to Me.

He had a Word for EVERYTHING.

My walk and my talks with Him in this season got me through some of the most intense moments I've ever had in my life. Looking now over this table of contents, from a distance, this looks like a person with real struggles.

That's me.
And probably you.

I experienced every single one of those spiritual and emotional emergencies in 2017.

Every.
Single.
One.

Maybe you're more put together or solid, but I'm real enough to say that I was on the struggle bus. As a matter of fact, for most of 2017, I was the driver, the tour guide, and the mechanic.

BUT HE HAD A WORD FOR ALL OF IT.

Usually, when I wrap the last page of a journal, it's no big thing to add it to the big leather white box with the rest of them, with a sense of accomplishment at having finished yet another segment of my story. Brushing off a new journal with a fresh set of pages ready for my precision pen brought a feeling of immense excitement, as it should! This is super easy...

Right?

It's just a book...put it in the box!

Right?

No. That was not at all how it worked this time.
I finished the last page of this particular journal, and then I wept.

I wept long and hard. The pages became crinkly and wet and I still wept.

I couldn't put it away! The thought of closing the lid on this journal felt like closing the lid of the casket on someone who bore my heart of hearts. It ripped my heart out to even consider it!

So I carried it around with me! Like a child, like a favorite handbag, like a wedding ring that never leaves your sight..I carried it around with me. In all of its completion, with no blank pages left, I carried it around with me, unsure as to why I couldn't put it away.

Until one day, I paged through this finished journal for a Word I knew was in there.

And He met me there. In the pages, He met me.

But this time, His Word to me was different:

> *Publish My glorious deeds among the nations. Tell everyone about the amazing things I have done. - 1 Chronicles 16:24-25 (NLT)*

And then there was:

> *Give thanks to Me and proclaim My greatness. Let the whole world know what I have done.*
> *- 1 Chronicles 16:8 (NLT)*

Oh and don't forget:

> *I have comforted you in all your troubles so that you can comfort others. When they are troubled, you will be able to give them the same comfort I have given you.*
> *- 2 Corinthians 1:4 (NLT)*

He says to me, CLEARLY:

> *YOU ARE SUPPOSED TO WRITE THIS BOOK.*

Now I'd love to say I jumped right on it, and I sat down like a good little Christian daughter of the King and pumped this book out like I was told.

But I didn't.

Distractions happened. Kids happened. Flu happened. Vacation happened. I happened.

But He kept telling me: Write the book. Write the book. Write the book. Through people, through Scripture, through music, through everything around me!

Write the book, Sabrina.

WHAT BOOK, LORD?

This book.
This is what He said:

> *I've given it to you already. It's your journal from this last year. Think about all that you dealt with. Pain and fear and rejection and failure and joy and sadness and loneliness and devastation and comparison and evil. Plenty and lack and hopes and dashed hopes. All of it. It's in there and we talked about it. Back and forth. Me and you. We talked it all through. You've got your manuscript already. It's your journal. My voice is in your journal. You wrote it all down. Now write it again, but this time for others. It's why you've been so heartbroken to put it away with the others now that you're done with it. You're not supposed to put it away. It's your book. It's OUR book.*

TEARS! All over again tears. It's why I couldn't put her away. It's my book.

It's OUR book.
It's YOUR book. YOURS. The person holding it and looking at these pages. It's your book.

So here it is.

My cries. Your cries. My fears. Your fears. My worries. Your worries.

All that I felt during that season is what many of you are feeling in your season.

And He's got a Word for ALL OF IT.

If you will just listen. He's got a Word.

I pray this book blesses you. It is directly from my journal in 2017. Every word of it. Use it when you're having an emergency, feeling some type of way, struggling in your faith, in your waiting, in your pain, in your loneliness, in whatever! He's got a Word. Share it with your friends and family, because they'll need it too. Make Him your go-to. He's always waiting on the other end.

The world offers a lot of go-tos when we are feeling bad. A lot of people to call or lots of places to post. Make Him your go-to. He's always on the other end.

He will never fail you.

Ever.

Faithfully Yours,

how to read this book

Consider this book to be very similar to a collection of conversations between you and God. Sort of like a compilation of 911 manuscripts for when you feel a certain way.

Every dialogue that you see within these pages lies within the pages of my journal. God's replies to me are based on actual Scripture. When I read the Bible, I love to draw from various translations, but you will find a good mix of my favorite three here: New Living Translation, The Message, and the New International Version. They are paraphrased in the voice of Him talking directly to me, and now to you.

Because His Word IS for me. And His Word IS for you. Personally.

I encourage you to visit the conversations as often as you need to, to commit the responses that speak to you the most to memory, and to even explore them further in the Bible. Skip around if you need to. It doesn't need to be read in consecutive order to be understood.

The Word is living and breathing, suiting every circumstance and speaking to every situation. It can speak to your heart just as it did to mine.

I felt EVERY SINGLE ONE of these chapters in 2017. God's Word was a soothing balm for all of it. Read it. Apply it to your individual circumstance. And do what it says.

His Word is true. And it works.

If we are willing to let it work.

PUBLISH MY GLORIOUS DEEDS AMONG THE NATIONS. TELL EVERYONE ABOUT THE AMAZING THINGS I HAVE DONE. — 1 CHRONICLES 16:24-25 (NLT)

GIVE THANKS TO ME AND PROCLAIM MY GREATNESS. LET THE WHOLE WORLD KNOW WHAT I HAVE DONE. — 1 CHRONICLES 16:8 (NLT)

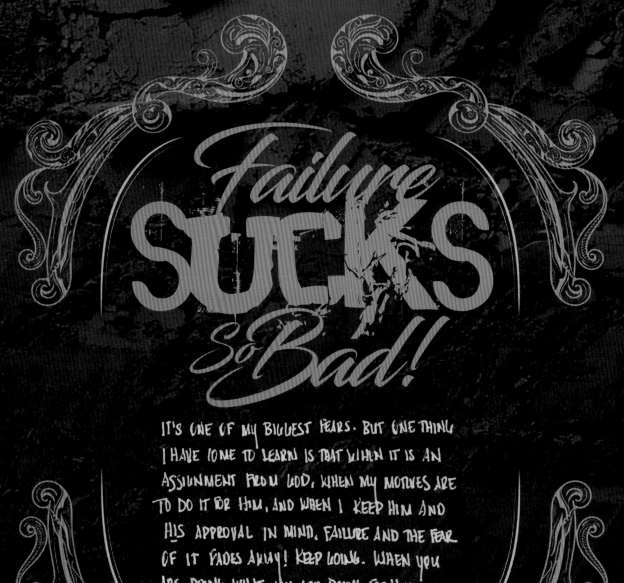

Failure SUCKS So Bad!

IT'S ONE OF MY BIGGEST FEARS. BUT ONE THING
I HAVE COME TO LEARN IS THAT WHEN IT IS AN
ASSIGNMENT FROM GOD, WHEN MY MOTIVES ARE
TO DO IT FOR HIM, AND WHEN I KEEP HIM AND
HIS APPROVAL IN MIND, FAILURE AND THE FEAR
OF IT FADES AWAY! KEEP GOING. WHEN YOU
ARE DOING WHAT YOU ARE DOING FOR HIM,
NOTHING ELSE MATTERS.

—SABRINA

Pick up the phone Lord...
I feel like a failure

Lord I have tried everything. I just can't get any of it to work. What am I doing wrong?

Search for Me. Search for Me continually. Continually seek Me and the strength you need to keep going. - Psalm 105:4 (NLT)

But God, did You hear me? I'm failing miserably. I just can't get it right!

Do not be discouraged, for I am your God. I will strengthen you and help you. I will hold you up with My victorious right hand. - Isaiah 41:10 (NLT)

Father, I am tired of trying. I've been trying so hard, yet nothing. Please help me.

I know all the things you do, and I have opened a door that no one can close. I know you have little strength, yet you obeyed Me and did not deny Me. - Revelation 3:8-10 (NLT)

So what if I try again, and fail again?

All things work together for your good because you love Me and have been called according to My purpose. - Romans 8:28 (NIV)

Okay I am willing Lord. Now what?

Trust in Me with all your heart and do not lean on your own understanding. In all your ways submit to Me and I will make your paths straight. - Proverbs 3:5-6 (NLT)

I believe You God. I am resolved to try again, as long as You are with me. I will try again.

Forget what is behind and strain towards what is ahead. Press on towards the goal to win the prize for which I have called you. - Philippians 3:13-14 (NIV)

Keep focused on your goal, if you want everything that I have for you. If you have anything else in mind, anything less than total commitment, I will clear your blurred vision - you will see it yet! So now that we are on the right track, stay on it!
- Philippians 3:15-17 (MSG)

Thank You Father. Okay. Here we go.

TRUST
HIM

I KNOW WHAT IT FEELS LIKE NOT TO KNOW. I AM THE QUEEN OF NEEDING ANSWERS.
BUT JUST TRUST HIM. HE'S GOT YOU. —SABRINA

Pick up the phone Lord... I don't know what to do

Lord God, is that You? I'm at my wit's end and I don't know what to do!

> *Be still, and know that I am God.*
> *- Psalm 46:10 (NIV)*

I hear You Lord, but that is so hard to do when things are happening and I just can't make sense of it all.

> *I am directing your steps. Why are you trying to understand everything along the way?*
> *- Proverbs 20:24 (NLT)*

Father, I am just at a loss. Please tell me what to do!

> *Seek Me and My Kingdom first, and live righteously, and I will give you everything you need. - Matthew 6:33 (NLT)*

Seek You first? What does that even mean? What does that look like?

> *Give thanks to Me and proclaim My greatness. Let the whole world know what I have done. Sing to Me, yes, sing My praises. Tell everyone about My wonderful deeds. Exult in My Holy Name. Rejoice, you who worships Me. Seek Me and My strength, continually. Remember the wonders I have performed, My miracles, and the rulings I have given. - Psalm 105:1-6 (NLT)*

Don't you understand that I need answers?

> *My thoughts are nothing like your thoughts, and My ways are far beyond anything you could imagine. - Isaiah 55:8 (NLT)*

> *I will guide you along the best pathway for your life. I will advise you and watch over you. - Psalm 32:8 (NLT)*

So what do I do? It's so hard not knowing.

> *Come to Me with ears wide open. Listen and you will find life. - Isaiah 55:3 (NLT)*

> *If you listen to Me and My instruction, you will prosper; if you trust in Me, you will be joyful. - Proverbs 16:20 (NLT)*

And what else: Besides seeking and listening?

> *Wait. Just wait quietly before Me. Because your hope is in Me and your victory comes from Me. - Psalm 62:1,5 (NLT)*

> *Trust Me more than you trust yourself.*
> *- Proverbs 3:5*

Pick up the phone Lord...
I'm so angry and cannot forgive

God, okay hear me out. I am so offended and so upset. I feel like I have every right to be so.

> *If it is possible, as far as it depends upon you, live at peace with everyone. - Romans 12:18 (NIV)*

But why do I need to forgive? Don't I have a right to be angry? Don't You understand?

> *I am gracious and compassionate, slow to anger and rich in love. I am good to all and I have compassion on all that I have made. - Psalm 145:8-9 (NIV)*

But I'm not You Lord. I'm so sorry if that sounds disrespectful. I have a hard time forgiving.

> *Again, I am compassionate and gracious, slow to anger, abounding in love. I do not always accuse, nor do I harbor my anger forever. I do not treat you as your sins deserve or repay you according to your iniquities.*
> *- Psalm 103:8-10 (NIV)*

I get all of that. Okay maybe just a firm word with them to get it off my chest?

> *Let no corrupt word proceed out of your mouth, but what is good for necessary edification, that it might impart grace to the hearers. - Ephesians 4:29 (NKJV)*

22

But I feel like I have a just fight! Are You asking me not to fight?

I, the Lord Myself, will fight for you. Just stay calm. - Exodus 14:14 (NLT)

So what am I supposed to do?

You are the light of the world, a town built on a hill that cannot be hidden. Let your light shine before others, that they may see your good deeds and glorify Me in Heaven. - Matthew 5:14,16 (NIV)

That's hard. I won't lie.

I, the God of endurance and encouragement, will help you live in complete harmony with others, as is fitting for My followers.
- Romans 15:5 (NLT)

Lord God, I hear You. But do You at least recognize how I feel?

Be glad and rejoice in My Love. I see your affliction and I know the anguish of your soul. I have not given you over into the hands of your enemy but have set your feet in a spacious place. - Psalm 31:7-8 (NLT)

Okay Lord. I believe You. I hear You. I know that You see me and feel me. I will try not to be angry. Help me to see them and forgive them as You do.

I will give you a new heart, and I will put a new spirit in you. I will take out your stubborn, stony heart and give you a tender, responsive heart.
- Ezekiel 36:26 (NLT)

I understand. I should forgive if I want to be more like You.

Be kind to them, tenderhearted, forgiving one another...

as I have forgiven you.

-Ephesians 4:32 (NLT)

Everyone hates me, and I think it's all Your fault

Lord, I'm sorry. I know this sounds crazy but I don't think anyone loves me. No calls, no texts, and I know it sounds dumb, but not many likes on social media these days. I feel so unwanted and disregarded. I think they all feel that I am annoying and don't care for me anymore.

I made you. I formed you in the womb. And I will help you. - Isaiah 44:2 (NIV)

I know that Lord. But I'm putting myself out there, with no response, just getting ignored. It makes me feel so invisible. Plus, I know in the back of my mind that people talk about me.

No one will be able to stand against you all the days of your life. As I was with Moses, so I will be with you. I will never leave you nor forsake you. - Joshua 1:5 (NIV)

So what do I do? Keep putting myself out there to be ignored and talked about in the background?

Serve wholeheartedly, as if serving for Me, not people, because you know I will reward each one for whatever good they do. - Ephesians 6:7-8 (NIV)

But Lord, it's so disheartening to think people actually hate me because of my love for You. How do I press through that?

Since it is through My mercy that you have this ministry, do not lose heart. - 2 Corinthians 4:1 (NIV)

I don't think You understand, Lord!

Everyone will hate you because of Me, but the one who stands firm will be saved. - Mark 13:13 (NIV)

I was rejected and despised by mankind, a man of suffering, and familiar with pain. Like one from whom people hide their faces I was despised, and held in low esteem. - Isaiah 53:3 (NIV)

I GET YOU.

Geez. So You do understand. All of this makes me feel foolish and ashamed but if You can do it, I will do it.

Instead of your shame, you will receive a double portion, and instead of disgrace you will rejoice in your inheritance. -Isaiah 61:7 (NIV)

So onward I go. Should I do anything about these people who slander me and are so mean to me?

You will not have to fight this battle. Take up your position, stand firm, and see the deliverance that I will give you. Do not be afraid; do not be discouraged. Go out and face them tomorrow and I will be with you. - 2 Chronicles 20:17 (NIV)

I Myself will fight for you.
JUST STAY CALM.
- Exodus 14:14 (NIV)

I, the Lord Myself, will

FIGHT FOR YOU.

Just stay calm.

EXODUS 14:14

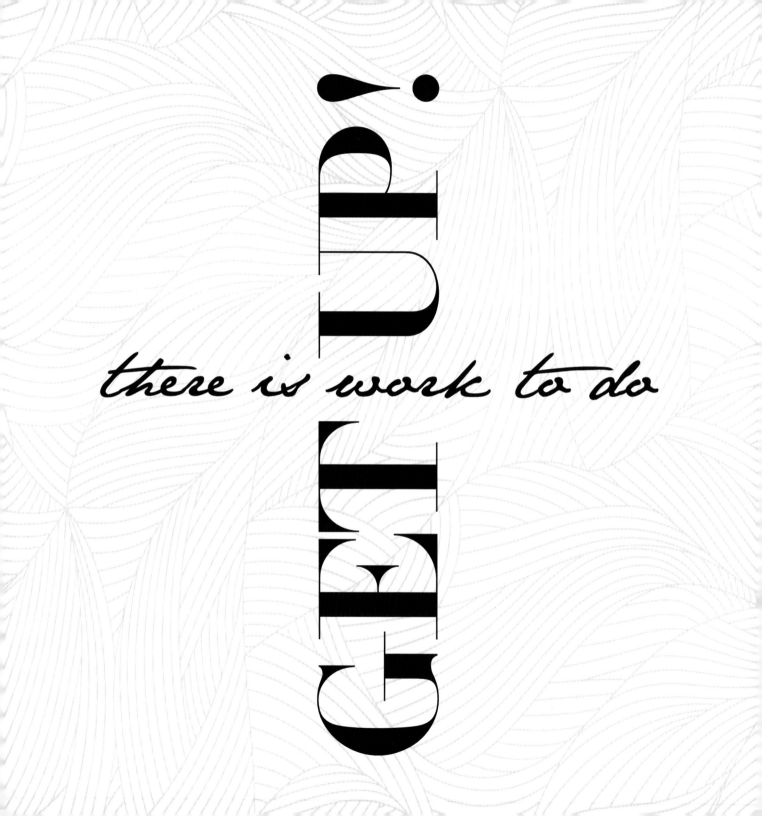

GET UP!

there is work to do

Pick up the phone Lord...
I'm down and can't pick myself up

Father, I've been down all day. Crying, laying in bed, and just feeling altogether sad. I just don't know how to get out of it.

> *In all things you are more than a conqueror through Me who loves you. - Romans 8:37 (NIV)*

It's too much! The sadness is just too much to bear! I don't know if I can conquer it!

> *You can do all of this through I who gives you strength. - Philippians 4:13 (NIV)*

I'm falling apart! A bucket of tears! And You just pretty much keep telling me to get over it?

> *Don't be dejected and sad, for My joy is your strength! - Nehemiah 8:10 (NLT)*

> *Your flesh and your heart may fail, but I am the strength of your heart and your portion forever. - Psalm 73:26 (NIV)*

I just don't know if I can get back up. Please help me to understand.

> *You are under great pressure, far beyond your ability to endure, so that you despair of life itself. Indeed, you feel as if you have received the sentence of death itself. But this happened that you might not rely on yourself, but on Me, who raises the dead. I have delivered you from such deadly peril, and I will deliver you again. Set your hope on Me that I will continue to deliver you.*
> *- 2 Corinthians 1:8-10 (NIV)*

I will try God. But the tears just keep flowing. It will be so hard.

> *Restrain your voice from weeping and your eyes from tears, for your work shall be rewarded. - Jeremiah 31:16 (NIV)*

I really just need a hug. I wish you could come here and hug me.

> *I am the God and Father of your Lord Jesus Christ, the Father of mercies and God of all comfort, who comforts you in your tribulation, that you may be able to comfort those with the comfort with which you yourself were comforted by Me.*
> *- 2 Corinthians 1:3-5 (NKJV)*

So what do I do? How do I take a first step out of this rut?

> *Whatever is true, whatever is noble, whatever is right, whatever is lovely, whatever is admirable, if anything is excellent or praiseworthy, think about such things. - Philippians 4:8 (NIV)*

> *You are the light of the world. A town on a hill cannot be hidden. Neither do people light a lamp and put it under a bowl. Instead they put it on its stand, and it gives light to everyone in the house. In the same way, let your light shine before others, that they may see your deeds and glorify Me.*
> *-Matthew 5:14-16 (NIV)*

Thank You Lord. If I am to show You to others, I guess I had better get out of this bed. Thank You for my hug. I love You.

Pick up the phone Lord... *I'm a horrible parent*

I'm giving it everything I've got Lord. But I feel like a horrible parent. I really am trying, but I just don't know where I'm going wrong.

> *I know your deeds, your hard work, and your perseverance. You have persevered and have endured hardships for My Name, and have not grown weary. - Revelation 2:2-3 (NIV)*

I've run out of parenting steam. I'm irritated all the time, short, and often harsh with them. I need Your help so badly.

> *So I say, walk by the Spirit. Let the Holy Spirit guide your life. Then you won't be doing what your sinful nature craves. The fruit of this Spirit is love, joy, peace, patience, kindness, goodness, faithfulness, gentleness, and self-control. - Galatians 5:16, 22-23 (NLT)*

I'm on E and that honestly sounds like more than I have left to give. But I guess I have to, right? They're my kids. I love them and I have to be there for them.

> *Be shepherds of My flock that is under your care, watching over them; not because you must, but because you are willing, as I want you to be. - 1 Peter 5:2 (NIV)*

I can't! How am I supposed to do that? I don't have it in me!

> *Greater am I that is in you, than he that is in the world. - 1 John 4:4 (NKJV)*

> *You can do all of this through Me who strengthens you. - Philippians 4:13 (NIV)*

So you're going to do this through me? You're going to have to. How does that work?

> *I must become greater. You must become less. - John 3:30 (NIV)*

I'm not doing anything wrong. At least I don't think I am. Yet my kids aren't responding. Will they be okay?

> *The righteous lead blameless lives. Blessed are their children after them. - Proverbs 20:7 (NIV)*

So You will help me?

> *All your children will be taught by Me, and great will be their peace. - Isaiah 54:13 (NIV)*

Thank You for encouraging me Lord. I just hope they get it.

> *Train them up in the way they should go, and even when they are old they will not depart from it. - Proverbs 22:6 (NKJV)*

Thank You Father. I give all that I am as a parent to You Lord. Thank You for Your help. I love You.

Greater

AM I THAT IS IN YOU,

THAN HE THAT IS

IN THE WORLD.

1 JOHN 4:4

NOTHING...

can ever separate you from My love.
Neither death nor life,
neither angels nor demons,
neither your fears for today
nor your worries about tomorrow -
not even the powers of hell
can separate you from My Love.
No power in the sky above or in the
earth below - indeed,
nothing in all creation will ever
be able to separate you
from my Love revealed
in my Son.

- Romans 8:38

Pick up the phone Lord... *I feel so alone*

Lord. I don't think I have ever felt so alone in my life. I've got so much I need to say, but no one to say it to. I can't really even call my parents or share with my husband. I just struggle alone.

I will not leave you orphans;
I will come to you. - John 14:18 (NKJV)

It makes me feel so bad. There are moments when I feel surrounded, wanted, and needed. And then there are moments when I just feel cast aside. No help. No checking on me. No nothing. Just discarded until I happen to pop up in someone's mind. I check on people all the time. I reach out all the time. I don't get any of it back.

I have chosen you and will not throw you
away. - Isaiah 41:9 (NLT)

It would be nice to have a people, a group, a squad, something! I don't know. Just folks who always notice if I'm not around or if I seem low. I don't know for sure if anyone notices or cares.

I will walk among you; I will be your God,
and you will be My people. - Lev 26:12 (NLT)

You're so busy God. I probably sound like a wimp. You probably don't have time for any of this.

Look up into the heavens. Who created all the
stars? I bring them out like an army, one after
another, calling each by its name. Because of
My great power and incomparable strength,
not a single one is missing. How can you say
that I do not see your troubles? How can you
say that I ignore your rights?
- Isaiah 40:26-27 (NLT)

I'm messed up with tears over here that You Lord, You who has to oversee all of this, have the time for ME, to make sure that I am seen to, and loved, and thought of. You don't forget me!

NEVER!
Can a mother forget her nursing child?
Can she feel no love for the child she has
borne? But even if that were possible, I would
not forget you! See I have written your name
on the palms of My hands.
- Isaiah 49:15-16 (NLT)

Lord, I can't tell You how much this comforts me. If I don't have anyone else, I have You.

Nothing can ever separate you from My love.
Neither death nor life, neither angels nor
demons, neither your fears for today nor your
worries about tomorrow - not even the powers
of hell can separate you from My Love. No
power in the sky above or in the earth below -
indeed, nothing in all creation will ever be
able to separate you from my Love revealed in
my Son. - Romans 8:38-39 (NLT)

I have called you by name.
You are mine.
- Isaiah 43:1 (NLT)

I want to try but I'm afraid of rejection

I'm mortified. I'm literally shaking in my boots. I know You've given me this thing to do, and I'm excited! But I'm terrified that no one will respond and that everyone will think it's garbage! I'm frozen with fear over it!

I, yes I, am the one who comforts you. So why are you afraid of mere humans, who wither like the grass and disappear? - Isaiah 51:12 (NLT)

I poured everything I have into this Lord. What if, after all of that, it still isn't received well? What if they don't think I have any idea what I'm talking about? What if they see me as deficient?

You are not qualified to do anything on our own. Your qualification comes from Me. - 2 Corinthians 3:5 (NLT)

But I need good feedback. I worry that I won't get any at all.

Don't put your trust in mere humans. They are as frail as breath. What good are they? - Isaiah 2:22 (NLT)

Maybe I should just wait. Maybe give it more time. Maybe tease them a little more and garner more excitement. Maybe I shouldn't go out on a limb with this at all. I know You've given me this responsibility, but maybe it's just not the right time? Ugh...Lord I'm a mess!

Because you understand your fearful responsibility to Me, work hard to persuade others. I know you are sincere, and they will know this, too. - 2 Corinthians 5:11 (NLT)

So I should go for it? Should I go over it again? Should I run it by someone else? And someone else after that? Should I rethink the whole thing?

Keep your message and preaching very plain. Rather than using clever and persuasive speeches, rely only on the power of the Holy Spirit. Do this so you would trust not in human wisdom but in My power. - 1 Corinthians 2:4-5 (NLT)

I hope You see me Lord. I'm doing it. And I'm doing it scared. But I'm doing it for You.

Instead of shame and dishonor, you will enjoy a double share of honor. You will possess a double portion of prosperity in your land, and everlasting joy will be yours. - Isaiah 61:7 (NLT)

DON'T PUT

YOUR TRUST IN

mere humans

THEY ARE AS

FRAIL AS

BREATH.

WHAT GOOD

ARE THEY?

ISAIAH 2:22

I WILL GIVE YOU A

new heart

AND I WILL

PUT A

NEW SPIRIT

IN YOU

EZEKIEL 36:26

Pick up the phone Lord...
I need a do-over
———➤

I messed up. I wish I could turn back time, but I know I can't. I wish I could have a redo. Maybe I'd think about things first, pray about them, maybe I wouldn't have botched this up so bad.

> *Anyone who belongs to Christ has become a new person. The old life is gone; a new life has begun!*
> *- 2 Corinthians 5:17 (NLT)*

But I messed up this time. I can't imagine how I can recover from this and even begin to make things right. I think I royally messed up the whole thing.

> *I, who began the good work within you, will continue My work until it is finally finished on the day when Christ Jesus returns. - Philippians 1:6 (NLT)*

What about where I messed up? Doesn't that just ruin everything?

> *I cause everything to work together for the good of those who love Me and are called according to My purpose for them. - Romans 8:28 (NLT)*

So You can even make my mess-ups become setups. Is that the truth? I know You can do that. But I'll always bear in mind how I ruined this whole chance. I think it just messes with my whole outlook on the situation. It's a real bummer. I want a do-over but I'm stuck between frustrated with myself and worried about doing it again! I've got issues Lord.

> *I will give you a new heart, and I will put a new spirit in you. I will take out your stony, stubborn heart and give you a tender, responsive heart. And I will put my Spirit in you so that you will follow my decrees and be careful to obey my regulations. - Ezekiel 36:26-27 (NLT)*

How can I be sure?! I want to believe that You can give me both a fresh start and a new outlook in my mind and in my situation. But how can I be sure?!

> *Look, I am making everything new! Write this down, for what I tell you is trustworthy and true.*
> *- Revelation 21:5 (NLT)*

I guess that's my Word. Okay....I messed up, but I'm going again. If You are willing to help me by making this new, I'm willing to use the fresh start to try again. Thank You Father for loving me so much. I love You.

My anxiety is going to kill me

Ughhhh Lord! So many things going on, so many people depending upon me, so many things to do, so much not happening the way I need it to, and I can't handle it all! My anxiety is on level 100. I'm in tears. I just can't manage everything. Please help me!

My dear. You are worried and upset over all of these details. There is only One Thing to be concerned about, and it will not be taken away from you. - Luke 10:41-42 (NLT)

That's so much easier said than done Lord. But "all of these details" won't just go away. How can I not worry? How will not worrying change the fact that this stuff is still staring at me?

Can all of your worries add a single moment to your life? - Matthew 6:27 (NLT)

No, they don't. If anything it feels like this anxiety is taking away moments of my life. What am I supposed to do? You make it sound so simple, but it's so difficult. What am I supposed to do?

Don't worry about anything; instead, pray about everything. Tell Me what you need, and thank Me for all I have done. Then you will experience My peace, which exceeds anything you can understand. My peace will guard your heart and mind as you live in Me. - Philippians 4:6-7 (NLT)

Lord, I don't think You really understand the magnitude of what I have facing me. It's so hard.

Give all your worries and cares to Me. I care about you. - 1 Peter 5:7 (NLT)

So step one in all of this. Giving my anxiety over to You is what? What does that look like? There's so much coming up. Where do I even begin?

Seek My Kingdom above all else, and live righteously, and I will give you everything you need. Don't worry about tomorrow, for tomorrow will bring its own worries. Today's trouble is enough for today. - Matthew 6:33-34 (NLT)

Seek You. Got it. Live a life that pleases You. Got it. Pray about everything and tell You what I need. Got it. Then what?

Be still. Know that I am God. - Psalm 46:10 (NLT)

Lord, I'm scared. That sounds amazing. And I know this sounds crazy, but I'm scared to not worry and not be anxious and to let go of all of this to trust You.

Be strong and courageous! Do not be afraid and do not panic. I will personally go ahead of you. I will neither fail you nor abandon you. - Deuteronomy 31:6 (NLT)

Deep breath...okay Lord. I trust You. You are so much bigger than I am and I know that You can do more with all of these things than I ever could. Thank You. I love You.

I am leaving you a gift - peace of mind and heart. And the peace I give is a gift the world cannot give. So don't be troubled. Do not be afraid. - John 14:27 (NLT)

TRUST ME.

" TRUST ME

MORE THAN YOU
TRUST YOURSELF "
PROVERBS 3:5

Pick up the phone Lord...
No one is supporting me

I put my heart out there Lord. I think I did a good job! I spent so much time and effort on this project...and crickets. I got a few responses from some faithful friends, but otherwise, nothing. It's left me feeling very dejected.

Do not let your heart be troubled. You trust in Me, right? - John 14:1 (NLT)

I do! But it's so embarrassing to put so much out there and no one shows up. How can I recover from this?

Because I help you, you will not be disgraced. Set your face like stone, determined to do My will. Know that you will not be put to shame. - Isaiah 50:7 (NLT)

Do you understand how it feels to be ignored? To be looked over even in my excitement? I feel so rejected right now.

I came into the very world I created, but the world didn't recognize Me. I came to My own people, and even they rejected Me. - John 1:10-11 (NLT)

Oh geez. That does give me a new outlook. It's very humbling to remember that if anyone understands rejection it's You. I needed that perspective as I've concentrated solely on me and that's probably where I've gone wrong. It's not about me. It's about You.

Humble yourself before Me, and I will lift you up in honor. - James 4:10 (NLT)

How do I move beyond this? I don't even want to try again. What if they don't support me yet again?

Work willingly at whatever you do, as though you were working for Me rather than for people. Remember that I will give you an inheritance as your reward, and that the Master you are serving is Me. - Colossians 3:23-24 (NLT)

Okay. It's for You. It's for You Lord. But please help me. Without You I don't think I can do it.

Ask Me to show you My approval and to make your efforts successful.
- Psalm 90:17 (NLT)

I Am all you need.

I AM
all you need

In your

DISTRESS

you cried out to Me;
yes, you prayed to Me for help.
I have heard you from My Sanctuary;
your cry to Me has reached My ears.

- Psalm 18:6

Pick up the phone Lord... I can't hear you

Father! I've called and cried and prayed and listened and nothing! I feel like You've gone silent on me! Do You hear me?? Please!

In your distress you cried out to Me; yes, you prayed to Me for help. I have heard you from My Sanctuary; your cry to Me has reached My ears. - Psalm 18:6 (NLT)

You heard me. But I cannot hear You. Am I missing something? Aren't I supposed to be able to hear You?

Ears to hear and eyes to see- both are gifts from Me. - Proverbs 20:12 (NLT)

I just don't know. I can't discern Your Voice. I feel like so many hear You so clearly. I long for that for myself. I desperately want to hear You.

You can be sure of this: I set apart the godly for Myself. I will answer when you call to Me. - Psalm 4:3 (NLT)

I've got so much going on. If I don't hear from You and hear from You soon, I don't know what I'll do.

Now I will take the load from your shoulders; I will free your hands from their heavy tasks. You cried to Me in trouble, and I saved you; I answered out of the thundercloud and tested your faith when there was no water at Meribah. - Psalm 81:6-7 (NLT)

How will I know I'm hearing from You? I don't want to miss a Word.

When the Spirit of truth comes, He will guide you into all truth. He will not speak on His own, but will tell you what He has heard. He will tell you about the future. He will bring Me glory by telling you whatever He receives from Me. - John 16:13-14 (NLT)

How will I know that I'm hearing You? I want to hear specifically. You spoke to Noah, Solomon, Abraham, all of those in specifics. I want that too. I don't want to take one step without hearing from You.

Your own ears will hear Me. Right behind you a voice will say, "This is the way you should go," whether to the right or to the left. - Isaiah 30:21 (NLT)

I don't want to miss You Lord. Not one Word. Please don't let me miss.

My child, pay attention to what I say. Listen carefully to My Words. Don't lose sight of them. Let them penetrate deep into your heart, for they bring life to those who find them, and healing to their whole body. - Proverbs 4:20-22 (NLT)

Okay I'm listening. I'm listening to every word and to every syllable; I am listening. I am open to whatever You have to say.

Come to Me with your ears wide open. Listen, and you will find life. - Isaiah 55:3 (NLT)

I'm here. I'm ready. And I'm listening.

I don't even know why I'm here

This may sound brutal God, but what's my point? I see so many other people getting big things done, accomplishing so much, having so much influence, and then there's me. I don't even know why I'm here. There's got to be more.

> *You are My masterpiece. I have created you anew in My Son, so that you can do the good things that I planned for you long ago. - Ephesians 2:10 (NLT)*

What things? Everyone has their thing. Everyone seems to know exactly what they like and what they are supposed to do. Accomplishing big things, super profitable, and celebrated. I'm working super hard, but I don't even know if this is my point here on the planet. Am I supposed to be doing something different? More like they are?

> *You are not like that, for you are a chosen people. You are a royal priest, a holy nation, My very own possession. As a result, you can show others My goodness, for I have called you out of the darkness into My wonderful light. - 1 Peter 2:9 (NLT)*

Royal priest? Did I sign up for that? Can I even do that? I don't know if that's what I meant.

> *You didn't choose Me. I chose you. I appointed you to go and produce lasting fruit, so that I will give you whatever you ask for, using My Name. - John 15:16 (NLT)*

Oh man that's huge. That's a huge responsibility. What if I can't do it. What if I can't step up to the plate on that? Will I lose my purpose?

> *My gifts and My call can never be withdrawn. - Romans 11:29 (NLT)*

That makes me feel amazing. I feel like a renewed call and passion has been placed on my life. It's sort of overwhelming! But in a good way of course. So I am here for You. To share You, Your love, and Your light. I do have a purpose! Thank you Father!

And remember...no eye has seen, no ear has heard, and no mind has imagined what I have prepared for those who love Me.
- 1 Corinthians 2:9 (NLT)

> *Now go. I have called you by name; for you are Mine. - Isaiah 43:1 (NLT)*

YOU DIDN'T CHOOSE ME...

I chose you

JOHN 15:16

Pick up the phone Lord...
I'm trying so hard to live right,
but I'm struggling

Okay Lord, hear me out. I love You. I do. I know what You have done for me, I'm so thankful, and I love You for it. But it's so hard to live right. Everyone is doing what they want, watching what they want, posting what they want, with no regard to what it looks like. Sometimes I feel like the oddball out trying to do the right thing and say the right thing all the time; especially when all I really want to do is the exact opposite sometimes. It's HARD! Why is it so easy for them, yet so difficult for me?

> *Those who are dominated by the sinful nature think about sinful things, but those who are controlled by the Holy Spirit think about things that please the Spirit. - Romans 8:5 (NLT)*

But I'm not perfect. I think of things that please the Spirit, but I'm not perfect. So it's not horribly bad that I fall in with those who choose not to live right on purpose sometimes, right?

> *But you are not controlled by your sinful nature. You are controlled by the Spirit if you have My Spirit living in you. (And remember that those who do not have My Spirit living in them do not belong to Me at all.) - Romans 8:9 (NLT)*

My sinful nature...it's always there. I know what You did for me to be free. But that doesn't make it all just up and go away. How do I resist that?

> *Letting your sinful nature control your mind leads to death. But letting the Spirit control your mind leads to life and peace. - Romans 8:6 (NLT)*

Geez. Looks like I have to battle against that nature just for peace. I didn't realize this would be so difficult. How does this affect anything else besides my peace?

> *My curse blights the house of the wicked, but I bless the home of the righteous. - Proverbs 3:33 (MSG)*

So it's basically impossible to say that I have Your Spirit in me, but to engage in a little recklessness every once in awhile on purpose? Is that what You're saying?

I am light, and there is no darkness in Me at all. You are lying if you say you have fellowship with Me but go on living in spiritual darkness; you are not practicing truth. - 1 John 1:5-6 (NLT)

LORD! But don't You know who I'm up against? He makes it so difficult! I want to react like You would, or to stay in my lane that honors You, but he just makes it so hard!

Look, I have given you authority over all the power of the enemy, and you can walk among snakes and scorpions and crush them. Nothing will injure you. - Luke 10:19 (NLT)

Put on all of My armor so that you will be able to stand firm against all the strategies of the devil. - Ephesians 6:11 (NLT)

You are right. I can do this. It's all for You after all. And not because I HAVE TO, but because I want to, to honor what You did for me. How do I even begin Lord?

You were taught to be made new in your thinking. You were taught to start living a new and holy life. It is created to be truly good and holy, just as I am. - Ephesians 4:23-24 (NIRV)

New thoughts. New attitudes. You're right. I can absolutely do this because You have made me new. This can't be as hard as I'm making it out to be.

Imitate Me, therefore, in everything you do, because you are My dear child. Live a life filled with love, following My Son's example. He loved you and offered Himself as a sacrifice for you, a pleasing aroma to Me. - Ephesians 5:1-2 (NLT)

I will do it for You. Jesus' sacrifice was too great a price to bear for me to not honor it with my life. I will do it Lord.

Let every detail in your life- words, actions, whatever- be done in the name of your Master Jesus, thanking Me, the Father, every step of the way. - Colossians 3:17 (MSG)

It is hard living for Christ. I get it. Social media lets people share what they want, post what they want, disrespect each other how they want, in a society that places little to no value on others' feelings. But, when we look at life through the lens of the high price that was paid for us, we should want to honor it by living lives that are a "pleasing aroma" to Him. A grand price was paid for us after all.

THE QUESTION IS, HOW WILL WE HONOR THAT?

PUT ON ALL OF

MY ARMOR

SO THAT YOU WILL BE ABLE TO STAND FIRM

AGAINST ALL THE STRATEGIES

OF THE DEVIL...

EPHESIANS 6:11

Pick up the phone Lord...
My faith is on its way out

God, I've been "faithing" it for so long. I know what You said. I've stayed in Your Word. I've prayed and I've fasted. I've kept my eyes on You. But I need a faith break. Do I ever get a chance to just rest in everything finally being alright for awhile? My faith is waning and there are so many things going on. I'm scared and faith just doesn't seem to be cutting anymore. How long do I have to do this? When will You show up?

> *If I care so wonderfully for flowers that are here today and thrown into the fire tomorrow, I will certainly care for you. Why do you have so little faith? - Luke 12:28 (NLT)*

I know you care for the flowers God. I'm not being ridiculous. But I'm a human. I'm a person. I am YOURS. I have feelings. There are so many things going on and my faith can only take so much. Do we ever get a reprieve?

> *Again I say: If I care so wonderfully for the wildflowers that are here today and thrown into the fire tomorrow, I will certainly care for you. WHY DO YOU HAVE SO LITTLE FAITH? - Matthew 6:30 (NLT)*

Wildflowers stand there! They don't have worries like I do! You created Me in Your own image. Don't You understand? Forgive my forwardness God, but I am just tired! I don't want to stand on faith anymore! I just want things to be okay for just a minute! I want to BREATHE!

> *Your faith is so small! Why are you so afraid! - Matthew 8:26 (NIRV)*

You don't hear me. The burden is so heavy. I've got so much to worry about. I'm trying to trust You, but there's always something. Something else at every turn. My faith is taking a severe beating and I just can't think about one more thing.

> *People who are ungodly run after all those things. I, your Father, know that you need them. But put My Kingdom first. Then those other things will also be given to you. - Luke 12:30-31 (NIRV)*

Lord. I'm tired. I just don't know what I'm supposed to have faith in anymore. You, of course. But what is the point of all of this pressing through. Is there a point to all of this? A purpose? I'm just tired.

> *Do not tremble; do not be afraid. Did I not proclaim My purposes for you long ago? - Isaiah 44:8 (NLT)*

You did. I know what Your Word says. I know Your Word says that You have a plan for me. I know that Your Word says You are going to do exceedingly over what I can imagine. I know that Your Word says no eye has seen what You have prepared for me. I know all of it. But with so much pressure, that Word, that faith, is just so hard to stand on. Do You hear me God? Does this make any sense at all?

> *But you must continue to believe this Truth and stand firmly on it. Don't drift away from the assurance you received when you heard the Good News. - Colossians 1:23 (NLT)*

It's hard. I want to continue to stand in faith, but it's hard. I find myself trying to figure out a way. But I know that's not the way either. It's just so hard God.

> *You must believe and not doubt, because the one who doubts should not expect to receive anything from Me. - James 1:6-7 (NIV)*

I want my faith to bear up God. I do. I want Your Word and Your promise to be all I need. I want to continue to believe You. I just need a sign, anything.

> *I have said what I would do, and I will do it. - Isaiah 46:11 (NLT)*

> *I am not a man, so I do not lie. I am not human, so I do not change My mind. Have I ever spoken and failed to act? Have I ever promised and not carried it through? - Numbers 23:19 (NLT)*

So I keep my faith, trusting You, Your Word, and Your promise. I'm tired. But either I believe You or I don't. I understand. There's got to be a reward for this severe faith walk, though, right?

> *When your faith is tested, your endurance has a chance to grow. So let it grow, for when your endurance is fully developed, you will be perfect and complete, needing nothing. - James 1: 3-4 (NLT)*

I hear You Lord.

> *I ask: Do you finally believe? - John 16:31 (NLT)*

I believe You. No matter what I believe You. I will keep my faith and believe You. With Your help, I can make it through. Breathing deep now. Thank You Lord. Here we go.

There were times when...

There were times when I felt beat down, run over, and mangled on this massive faith walk I've been on. I understand being weak in the faith knees. It's one of the worst feelings ever. But God's word never changes.

His faithfulness does not bow and dip like ours. We can count on Him! No matter what it takes: if you have to pray and fast often, if you have to get trusted friends to shore your arms up like Aaron and Ur did for Moses, if you have to cry out in your weakness, or if you have to read this a million times a day,

 STAY THE FAITH COURSE.

He is faithful my friend, just stay the course. Prayers up for you. You are not alone.

...ED ON THIS MASSIVE FAITH WALK, I'VE BEEN ON. I UNDERSTAND

...RE TIMES WHEN I FELT BEAT DOWN, RAN OVER, AND

BEING WEAK IN THE FAITH KNEES. IT'S ONE OF THE WORST FEELINGS EVER.

BUT GOD'S WORD NEVER CHANGES.

HIS FAITHFULNESS DOES NOT BOW AND DIP LIKE GUYS WE CAN COUNT ON TODAY.

NO MATTER WHAT IT TAKES. IF YOU HAVE TO PRAY AND FAST OFTEN,

IF YOU HAVE TO GET TRUSTED FRIENDS TO SHORE YOUR ARMS UP

LIKE AARON AND UR DID FOR MOSES. IF YOU HAVE TO CRY OUT IN YOUR

WEAKNESS, OR IF YOU HAVE TO READ THIS A MILLION TIMES A DAY.

STAY THE FAITH COURSE.

HE IS FAITHFUL MY FRIEND. JUST STAY THE COURSE. PRAYERS UP FOR YOU.

YOU ARE NOT ALONE.

Pick up the phone Lord... *I feel so unloved*

My phone hasn't rung in days. Unless I think of something attention-grabbing to post on Facebook, I think people just scroll on by. My kids are in their own corners, friends are busy with their own lives. I would love to hear someone intentionally reach out to me and just simply say I love you. I feel forgotten.

> *Never! Can a mother forget her nursing child? Can she feel no love for the child she has borne? But even if that were possible, I would not forget you! See, I have written your name on the palms of My hands. - Isaiah 49:15-16 (NLT)*

But You are God. You're supposed to love me. I'm talking about human love. I feel left out, neglected, unloved.

> *From eternity to eternity I AM God. No one can snatch you out of My hand. - Isaiah 43:13 (NLT)*

I know. I know. You love Me. It just feels like everyone has their lives, their busyness, their distractions that keep them from spending face time and pouring into each other. It leaves people like me sort of left behind. So much busyness. So much going on. I can't even compete. Who am I to ask for time when so much is happening that takes priority?

> *Even if the mountains walk away and the hills fall to pieces, My love won't walk away from you. - Isaiah 54:10 (MSG)*

Even You Lord. How can you love me so fiercely when there are so many others You have to love? It's amazing to me that You have time to single me out. It makes my heart explode.

> *You are precious to me. You are honored, and I love you. - Isaiah 43:4 (NLT)*

Okay You got me. Now my journal is all wet. I love You too God. I really do. Sometimes I find it so hard to believe just how much You do love me...or all of us. We are so bad sometimes!

> *May you have the power to understand, as all My people should, how wide, how long, how high, and how deep My love is. - Ephesians 3:18 (NLT)*

You are amazing God. Why do I feel so badly about this, when I should be basking in this great love I know You have for me. In spite of all I do and put You through, You always love me.

Nothing can ever separate you from My love. Neither death nor life, neither angels nor demons, neither your fears for today nor your worries about tomorrow – not even the powers of hell can separate you from My love. No power in the sky above or in the earth below – indeed, nothing in all creation will ever be able to separate You from My love that is revealed in Christ Jesus your Lord. - Romans 8:38-39 (NLT)

That kind of love I should never expect from my people I know. It's not possible for them to love me in that way. You love me so much. It has turned my whole mood around to be reminded of that. Thank You Lord.

No one has greater love than the one who gives their life for their friends.
- John 15:13 (NIRV)

I showed My great love for you by sending Christ to die for you while you were still a sinner. - Romans 5:8 (NLT)

I died for you. That is how much I love you.

I feel like I'm drowning and I'm so overwhelmed

God PLEASE! There is one thing after another after another. The moment I feel like I am on solid ground, there is something else. I am so discouraged and overwhelmed. Drowning in all that there is to do, all of the people I have to answer to, and all of the hopes I have that distress me. Are You there Lord? I don't know that I can bear it all. I almost wish You would just come back now so I don't have to think about any of it anymore. Please Father help me! Are you there?

> *In your distress you have cried out to Me; prayed to Me for help. I have heard you from My Sanctuary; your cry to Me has reached My ears. - Psalm 18:6 (NLT)*

Father I don't even have enough words to describe the burden I feel. I feel so broken and unable to carry any of it anymore. It's all just too much. I know You said You would never give us more than we can bear, but I feel as if I am dying beneath it all.

> *It is so bad you don't think you're going to make it. You feel like you've been sent to death row, that it is all over for you. As it turns out this is the best thing that could have happened. Instead of trusting in your own strength or wits to get out of it, you are forced to trust Me totally-not a bad idea since I Am the God who raises the dead! And I did it, rescued you from certain doom. And I'll do it again, rescuing you as many times as you need rescuing. - 2 Corinthians 1:8-10 (MSG)*

Trust is great, but I have been trusting my way through a lot of things. But that doesn't mean any of the everyday worry or stress goes away. Every single day, I bear all of this. How can trust help me with that? I am even beginning to feel it physically. Lord I feel like I'm dying slowly under the weight of it all!

> *That is why I tell you not to worry about everyday life- whether you have enough food and drink, or enough clothes to wear. Isn't life more than food, and your body more than clothing? Can all your worries add a single moment to your life?*
> *- Matthew 6:25, 27 (NLT)*

Please don't say I told you so Father. I just need Your help. I'm drowning under the pressure of it all. I don't think I can breathe with the burden.

> *I have reached down from heaven and rescued you; I have drawn you out of the deep waters. - Psalm 18:16 (NLT)*

I feel You near Lord. I just don't know what I am supposed to do to breathe again.

> *As pressure and stress bear down on you, find joy in My commands.*
> *- Psalm 119:143 (NLT)*

> *Give your burdens to Me, and I will take care of you. I will not permit you to slip and fall. - Psalm 55:22 (NLT)*

Lord I am terribly afraid. I know You are there. I know You are here to help me. But there's just so much. Lord there's just so much. But you already know that, I know.

> *I will keep you in perfect peace if you trust in Me; you whose thoughts are fixed on Me.*
> *- Isaiah 26:3 (NLT)*

Is there any end in sight? Is it horrible to long for relief?

> *Be truly glad. There is wonderful joy ahead, even though you must endure many trials for a little while. These trials will show that your faith is genuine. It is being tested as fire tests and purifies gold- though your faith is far more precious than mere gold. And when your faith remains strong through many trials, it will bring you much praise and glory and honor on the day when My Son is revealed to the whole world.*
> *- 1 Peter 1:6-7 (NLT)*

That's a lot to ask Father. I'm doing the best I can. You can see that I am here seeking YOU for my help. But you tell me that there are more trials? I'm doing the best I can to look to You, but this is horribly difficult. Has my faith not proven itself yet?

> *I will faithfully reward my people for their suffering and make an everlasting covenant with them. - Isaiah 61:8 (NLT)*

Reward sounds amazing. I long for that. I long for the finish line. I will try my hardest to keep going. I know it is important that I keep going. I talk about You a lot. If I cannot keep going, how can I expect others to?

> *Since you are surrounded by such a huge crowd of witnesses to the life of faith, strip off every weight that slows you down, especially the sin that so easily trips you up. Run with endurance the race that I have set before you by keeping your eyes on Jesus, the champion who initiates and perfects your faith. - Hebrews 12:1-2 (NLT)*

You're right. This talk alone helped me to find my breath. One thing, one person, one problem, one issue at a time. There's way too much to lose to give up now. And you are right, people are watching. I have to do this, if anything for those who look to me, like my kids and my husband. I have to do this.

> *So take a new grip with your tired hands and strengthen your weak knees. Mark out a straight path for your feet so that those who are weak and lame will not fall but become strong. - Hebrews 12:12-13 (NLT)*

I cannot do anything of this without You. Thank you for reaching down and taking ahold of me God. Without You I would indeed drown. But You are here. Thank You.

LIFE

Life isn't without its problems. Even with the perfect worlds that social media shows us sometimes, from the outside looking in, there are almost always things lurking beneath. Life will swallow us whole if we don't have a source for help. We can't do any of this alone. He is there, waiting to take ahold of you when things are closing in. All you have to do is call him. Trust me, I know. Praying for you always. There is an end to it all. You will breathe again.

Pick up the phone Lord...
My enemies are attacking me

Okay Lord. I'm trying to hold my tongue. I'm trying to show You in everything I do and everything I say. But sometimes people make it hard! How is it possible to be so mean, to attack someone, when all they do is show light and show YOU! Am I alone in being messed with even when I only stand for peace, love, and grace?

Don't worry about it- there are more on your side than on their side. - 2 Kings 6:16 (MSG)

Excuse my casual speech Father, but it almost feels like they believe I'm soft or naive because I stay on the side of what pleases You versus getting riled up. But there is only so much a body can take! I don't know if they know how close I am to losing my temper! Why should I continue to show grace to people who continue to attack me?

Count yourself blessed every time people put you down or throw you out or speak lies about you to discredit me. What it means is that the Truth is too close for comfort and they are uncomfortable. You can be glad when that happens- give a cheer, even!- for though they don't like it, I do! And all heaven applauds. And know that you are in good company. My prophets and witnesses have always gotten into this kind of trouble. - Matthew 5:11-12 (MSG)

They don't understand. They clearly don't know You or they wouldn't be this way. It messes with me so bad. My temper is still there and I want to defend myself. They pull me so close to losing it sometimes!

Be careful to live properly among your unbelieving neighbors. Then even if they accuse you of doing wrong, they will see your honorable behavior, and they will give honor to Me when I judge the world. - 1 Peter 2:12 (NLT)

You're asking a lot God.

I have called you to do good, even it means suffering, just as My Son suffered for you. He is your example, and you must follow in His steps. He never sinned, nor ever deceived anyone. He did not retaliate when He was insulted, nor threaten revenge when He suffered. He left His case in My hands, and I always judge fairly. - 1 Peter 2:21-23 (NLT)

So I am supposed to just let them mistreat me? Stand alone and let them attack, lie, and talk about me?

The Lord of Heaven's Armies is here among you; I, the God of Israel, am your fortress. - Psalm 46:11 (NLT)

So what do I do while I still stand for You? And what am I supposed to do if they continue their craziness against Me?

No weapon turned against you will succeed. You will silence every voice raised up to accuse you. These benefits are enjoyed by My servants; your vindication will come from Me. I, the Lord, have spoken! - Isaiah 54:17 (NLT)

58

I'm trusting You with my name Father, with my reputation and with my character. Because I know they talk about me, plot against me, make fun of me, and more. But I am trusting in what You tell me to do. Because no one's opinion or approval matters more to me than Yours.

My way is perfect. All of My promises prove true. I am a shield for all who look to Me for protection. I have subdued your enemies under your feet. I will hold you safe beyond the reach of your enemies, and save you from violent opponents.
- Psalm 18:30,39,48 (NLT)

Do not be afraid or discouraged. The battle is not yours, but Mine.
- 2 Chronicles 20:15 (NIV)

I will fight for you. You need only be still.
- Exodus 14:14 (NIV)

NO WEAPON
TURNED AGAINST YOU WILL SUCCEED

ISAIAH 54:17

SO I AM SUPPOSED TO JUST LET THEM MISTREAT ME?

STAND ALONE AND LET THEM ATTACK, LIE, AND TALK ABOUT ME?

THE LORD OF HEAVEN'S ARMIES IS HERE AMONG YOU; I, THE GOD OF ISRAEL, AM YOUR FORTRESS

Pick up the phone Lord...
I've sinned and feel so ashamed

It's being weighing on me all day Father and I'm so ashamed. I've sinned and I feel so ashamed. I know You already know what I've done, but yet it is still so hard to even stand before You because I know better and I know I've disappointed you.

There is no condemnation for those who belong to Christ Jesus. - Romans 8:1 (NLT)

That makes my heart melt a million times over because I know You don't condemn me! Jesus died for me! He was tortured for Me! For my sins! Yet I keep on doing things, even without realizing sometimes, and it rips my heart out because of the price paid for me.

Who dares accuse you whom I have chosen for My own? No one- for I Myself have given you right standing with Me. Who will then condemn you? No one- for My Son died for you and was raised to life for you, and He is sitting in the place of honor at My right hand, pleading for you. - Romans 8:33-34 (NLT)

He died for me, yet He still pleads for me! That breaks me Lord! I want to do better before You and to honor Your sacrifice! This sin of mine just ruins all of it!

I, yes, I alone- will blot out your sins for My own Name's sake and will never think of them again. - Isaiah 43:25 (NLT)

You just blot them out? I sin and You just never think of them again? That's so unreal to me Lord. I cannot believe that You have such love for me, even in my sinful state. I just can't process that Lord. My sin makes me want to hide from You, just like Adam and Eve did. It brings me shame, but yet You say You never think of them again. Who does that?

Who is a God like Me? I forgive sin. I forgive My people when they do what is wrong. I don't stay angry forever. Instead, I take delight in showing My faithful love to them. - Micah 7:18 (NIRV)

No one. No one is like you. I just can't believe You have such great love for me that You would just cast aside what I have done.

I say again, I will forgive your wickedness, and I will never again remember your sins. - Hebrews 8:12 (NLT)

Thank You Lord for what You are to me, for what You have done for me, and for how You love me. I feel like I can hold my face up to You now.

I've wiped the slate of all your wrongdoings. There's nothing left of your sins. Come back to me, come back. I've redeemed you. - Isaiah 44:22 (MSG)

Pick up the phone Lord...
Everyone else is doing great but me

I know the Truth. I know what You say about me: that I am Your beloved, that I am blessed and highly favored, that I have been called by name...but I look around and I just get downright envious. It's shameful I know. But I watch other people doing so much, accomplishing so much, having letters behind their names, or sharing their #relationshipgoals, or traveling and seeing the world, or being the perfect parent with perfect kids, or buying new homes and things, and...

You get it Lord. I know my eyes have strayed. But I can't help thinking...they are all doing so much more than I am and sometimes I just wish it were me.

> *You are My masterpiece. I have created you anew in Christ Jesus, so that you can do the good things I planned for you long ago. - Ephesians 2:10 (NLT)*

See I KNOW that. I guess it's just hard. The flesh part of me wants so many things, for myself and for my loved ones. I'm just not in the position others are to be able to have these types of blessings or to even be able to bless others the way I want to. It probably sounds so dumb, and so ungrateful, but I'm just being honest with You. I know You already know.

> *I am able, through My mighty power at work within you, to accomplish infinitely more than you might ask or think.*
> *- Ephesians 3:20 (NLT)*

I guess it's just hard not to be covetous sometimes. Or just to make it plain...jealous. Some of these folks you just can't help but to watch them and want.

> *Don't evaluate people by what they have or how they look. - 2 Corinthians 5:16 (MSG)*

> *Among you it will be different. If you want to be a leader, you must be a servant, and if you want to be first you must become a slave. For even My Son came not to be served, but to serve others and to give His life as a ransom for many.*
> *- Matthew 20:26-28 (NLT)*

So basically, I may or may not achieve such big things in life and have amazing things like some. But my entire purpose is to serve. That sounds hard. And if I'm to be honest, it makes me a bit sad. Some of these people could care less about You, but they have everything. Those of us who have dedicated our lives to You, we get to go without. That makes me sad. How do they benefit from unbelief, but we get to struggle despite our belief?

Make Me truly happy by agreeing wholeheartedly with others, loving others, and working together with one mind and purpose. Don't be selfish; don't try to to impress others. Be humble, thinking of others as better than yourself. Don't look out only for your own interests, but take an interest in others, too. You must have the same attitude that My Son had.
- Philippians 2:2-5 (NLT)

And just like that, I am severely reminded of Jesus. He could have had all the world if He wanted. He could have done, or become, or taken for Himself, anything He wanted. But He did not. He lived a life of service to ME so that I might be saved, thus I should do the same. I am humbled beyond belief at my selfishness. I just work really hard to share You with others and I struggle sometimes with seeing others who don't love you like I do just living it up without a care. But I will keep working, and I will keep my eyes on You. You are all that matters.

Your work might seem so useless. You may feel as if you have spent your strength for nothing and to no purpose. Leave it all in My hand; trust Me for your reward. Those who trust in Me will never be put to shame. - Isaiah 49:4,23 (NLT)

The fact that You see me Lord is enough. That is enough for me. Thank You for seeing me. Thank You for hearing me and listening without judging me. No matter what others have, or accomplish, or do, I know that You see me. I know that You love me.

And that is enough for me.

Social media. Social media makes it so hard. The physique. The hand-selected filters make us wish we our "friends" are having and "checking-in" to all has allowed us to peek into others' worlds what we don't have, who we wish we were, and get caught up in the 'I wish that were me' syndrome. Real and there are many of us who struggle from even to yourselves. God has a plan and a just reward eyes on others. Keep your eyes heavenward, seeking all your eyes cannot see and your mind just cannot

PERFECTLY STAGED SELFIES CAUSE US TO ENVY OTHERS' STYLE AND

WERE HAVING AS MUCH OF A DELIRIOUSLY GOOD TIME AS

THE FUN AND EXOTIC PLACES THEY GET TO GO. SOCIAL MEDIA

AND MOST OF THE TIME, SEE THEM THROUGH THE EYES OF

WHAT IS MISSING FROM OUR OWN LIVES. IT IS SO EASY TO

IF THAT ISN'T YOU, KUDOS. BUT THIS BOOK KEEPS IT VERY

TIME TO TIME. SO FOR THOSE OF WHOM ARE WILLING TO ADMIT IT...

FOR EACH OF US. DON'T LOSE FOCUS ON THAT BY KEEPING YOUR

THAT HE HAS PLANNED JUST FOR YOU.

IMAGINE HOW WONDERFUL IT WILL BE. — SABRINA

DO YOU *believe* NOW? JOHN 16:31

YES FATHER. I BELIEVE. THANK YOU FOR PICKING ME UP.

Pick up the phone Lord... *I'm so discouraged*

I'm doing everything right. I know I am. But yet, nothing progresses. Nothing moves. Nothing improves. I want to just throw in the towel God! It's always something! I'm so discouraged!

Do not fear, for I am with you; do not be dismayed, for I am your God. I will strengthen you and help you; I will uphold you with My righteous right hand.
- Isaiah 41:10 (NIV)

I know You are there, but with every waking moment I'm just not sure we will ever move forward. I'm beginning to doubt all of it!

When doubts filled your mind, My comfort will give you renewed hope and cheer.
- Psalm 94:19 (NLT)

So many people are expecting so much of me. It's so embarrassing to have nothing to show them. I'm so embarrassed, but I know You have something big. How do I keep going when things just don't seem to be happening?

Because I, your Sovereign Lord, help you, you will not be disgraced. Therefore, set your face like stone, determined to do My will. And know that you will not be put to shame. - Isaiah 50:7 (NLT)

I just don't know. Maybe I should throw in the towel and try a new approach. Walk away from it all and do something different. There's just one obstacle after another. I know You have a plan. But it's so hard to see it with all that is in the way.

Don't ever give up. Your present troubles are small and won't last very long. They will produce for you a glory that vastly outweighs them and will last forever! Don't look at the troubles you can see now; rather, fix your gaze on things that cannot be seen. For the things you see now will soon be gone, but the things you cannot see will last forever. - 2 Corinthians 4:16-18 (NLT)

This is My command- be strong and courageous! Do not be afraid or discouraged. For I Am with you wherever you go. - Joshua 1:9 (NLT)

I believe You. Or at least I'm trying to.

I will help your overcome your unbelief.
- Mark 9:24 (NLT)

Look, I Am making everything new! Write this down. You can trust these words. They are true. - Revelation 21:5 (NIRV)

I feel unappreciated

I put a lot of effort and work into what I'm doing. But I honestly don't think anyone sees, cares, or appreciates it. People just take advantage and for the most part, I never get a thank you or an acknowledgment or anything. How do I deal with what I'm feeling?

Be like the Son of Man. He did not come to be served. Instead, He came to serve others. He came to give His life as the price for setting many people free.. - Matthew 20:28 (NIRV)

You must have the same attitude that Christ Jesus had. - Philippians 2:5 (NLT)

But Lord, I'm putting in major work! How am I supposed to do that? It's hard doing this day in and day out just to think that no one cares! It makes you want to just stop!

Don't get tired of doing what is good. At just the right time you will reap a harvest of blessing if you don't give up. - Galatians 6:9 (NLT)

But do You at least see how much work I'm putting in?

I know what you are doing. You work long and hard. You have been faithful and have put up with a lot of trouble because of Me. You have not given up. - Revelation 2:2-3 (NIRV)

How am I supposed to keep going if no one ever acknowledges what I'm doing? It's hard.

I am working in you. I want your plans and your acts to fulfill My good purpose. Do everything without complaining or arguing. - Philippians 2:13-14 (NIRV)

You can do all this by the power of Christ. I give you strength. - Philippians 4:13 (NIRV)

I hope no one can tell how I feel. I know that I can talk to you about it. I really want to keep serving, to keep proclaiming, and to keep sharing You, but I hope my attitude doesn't reflect that I feel unappreciated.

Let everyone see that you are considerate in all you do. Remember, I Am coming soon. - Philippians 4:5 (NLT)

So what do I do?

Work willingly at whatever you do, as though you were working for Me rather than for people. - Colossians 3:23 (NLT)

Because I see you.
- Genesis 16:13

YOU MUST HAVE THE SAME

attitude

THAT CHRIST JESUS HAD.

PHILIPPIANS 2:5

Pick up the phone Lord...
My situation feels so hopeless

I've reached the end of myself Lord. I cannot come up with any solutions, ideas, or even a place to start over. If there was ever such a thing as the bottom of the hope pit, I'm there. I can't fix this if I tried. My problems are so big right now and I have no idea where to start. Without You I am doomed.

I know the plans I have for you. They are plans for good and not for disaster, to give you a future and a hope. When you pray, I will listen. - Jeremiah 29:11-12 (NLT)

I know Your Word. I know THAT Word. But right now, it just doesn't seem to make sense with my situation. None of this is good. None of this has hope. All of it seems disastrous. How can I rely on that Word with everything I can see?

My Word will never fail. - Luke 1:37 (NLT)

Father please! Sticking with what I know Your Word says seems so hard, when my eyes tell me something different! There's so much and so little hope for all of it! How long before you unveil this plan You have for me??

Your present troubles are small and won't last very long. Yet they produce for you a glory that vastly outweighs them and will last forever! - 2 Corinthians 4:17 (NLT)

Not very long...but some of this stuff is so bad. I just can't see a way past it. What about those things?

I cause everything to work together for the good of those who love Me and are called according to My purpose for them. - Romans 8:28 (NLT)

If I were to list it all, no one would believe what I'm dealing with. I just don't know how these things will pull together or even how I'll pull out of them. It's just so much. One thing after another after another. I'm so bowed down under them all.

No, despite all these things, overwhelming victory is yours through Christ, who loves you. - Romans 8:37 (NLT)

Forget the things that happened in the past. Do not keep on thinking about them. I am about to do something new. It is beginning to happen even now. Don't you see it coming? I am going to make a way for you to go through the desert. I will make streams of water in the dry and empty land. - Isaiah 43:18-19 (NIRV)

I believe You God. But for all of this to work together, for all of this to see me emerge victorious, for all of this to produce glory...it seems impossible.

Humanly speaking, it is impossible. But with Me everything is possible. - Matthew 19:26 (NLT)

Who can do this? How can I do this?

Even when there was no reason for hope, Abraham kept hoping- believing that he would become the father of many nations. For I had said to him, "That's how many descendants you will have!" And Abraham's faith did not weaken, even though, at about 100 years of age, he figured his body was as good as dead- and so was Sarah's womb. Abraham never wavered in believing My promise. In fact, his faith grew stronger, and in this he brought glory to Me. He was fully convinced that I was able to do whatever I promise. - Romans 4:18-21 (NLT)

That was Abraham back then. I am me, thousands of years later.

The God that Abraham believed in gives life to the dead. Abraham's God also creates things that did not exist before. - Romans 4:17 (NIRV)

I Am the same yesterday, today, and forever. - Hebrews 13:8 (NLT)

You will be blessed if you believe that I will fulfill My promise to you. - Luke 1:45 (NIV)

I will believe you.

With everything I have I will believe you.

I do not have a choice as You are my only hope.

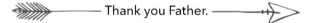 —— Thank you Father. ——

I AM THE SAME YESTERDAY, TODAY, AND FOREVER. - HEBREWS 13:8

Pick up the phone Lord... *I'm in so much pain*

My heart is broken Father. I feel so many emotions I can't explain them all. It's brutalizing that someone has the power and the ability to break your heart so badly. Crying out to You today because I just don't have human words to explain to anyone here how painful it feels.

I am close to those whose hearts have been broken. I save those whose spirits have been crushed. - Psalm 34:18 (NIRV)

I don't know how I can get over this. The pain is immense and I don't know how I'll recover, how I will look them in the eye and trust again, or how I can see them the same. The pain is real.

You are pressed on every side by troubles, but you are not crushed. You are perplexed, but not driven to despair. You are hunted down, but never abandoned by Me. You got knocked down, but you are not destroyed. - 2 Corinthians 4:8-9 (NLT)

I don't think I've ever felt this kind of pain before.

What you suffer now is nothing compared to the glory I will reveal to you later. - Romans 8:18 (NLT)

And it's really hard because I don't want to burden any of my people with it. I feel so alone in this pain and I can't talk to anyone about it.

I hold you by your right hand- I, the Lord your God. And I say to you, 'Don't be afraid. I am here to help you.' - Isaiah 41:13 (NLT)

You're always here for me. That just makes my heart explode.

You face many troubles, but I rescue you each time. I protect the bones of the righteous; not one of them is broken! - Psalm 34:19-20 (NLT)

You are all I have Father. I know when everything shakes out, if no one else is there, if no one else understands, if no one else wants to listen, that You are there. Please help me to heal from this heart pain. I need You like never before if I am to move past this.

My grace is all you need. My power works best in weakness. Boast about your weaknesses, so that the power of Christ can work through you. Take pleasure in your weaknesses, and in the insults, hardships, persecutions, and troubles that you suffer for Christ. For when you are weak, then I am strong. - 2 Corinthians 12:9-10 (NLT)

Your flesh and your heart may fail, but I am the strength of your heart and your portion forever. - Psalm 73:26 (NIV)

I am brought low Father.

And I still love you, even at your darkest. You are mine. Come to Me, and I will give you rest. - Isaiah 43:1 & Romans 5:8 & Matthew 11:28

Pain is Real. Heartbreak is Real.
Whether it is grieving the physical loss or the emotional loss
of another, or working through a grievous offense by someone
who held your heart close, pain is real and it can be brutal. I would
love to say that having this conversation with God about this
type of pain just makes it all go away, but that would be a heinous lie.

 ———— Pain is a Process. ————→

But walking with God through that process will make it easier. He
not only feels your pain, but He knows your pain, better than
anyone. Be open and honest with Him. Give Him a shot to
help you heal. He can do it for you.

Pick up the phone Lord...
I'm down to my very last

Father I am coming to You humbly. I just don't have what I need. I am down to my last and I couldn't make what I'm missing appear if I tried. I desperately need Your help.

>*Put My Kingdom first. Do what I want you to do. Then all those things will also be given to you.*
>*- Matthew 6:33 (NIRV)*

I am Father, but that doesn't make my needs go away. I hope that doesn't sound disrespectful. I hope You see my heart. God, I am seeking and putting You first, but I still have these responsibilities to meet. I still have great need. It worries me so bad.

>*I will meet all your needs. I will meet them in keeping with My wonderful riches. These riches come to you because you belong to Christ Jesus. - Philippians 4:19 (NIRV)*

I love You with everything I have Lord God! I long for You and I can't live without You, but I have very real needs right now and I don't know where it is to come from!

>*Even though the fig trees have no blossoms, and there are no grapes on your vines; even though your olive crop fails, and your fields lie empty and barren; even though the flocks die in your fields, and your cattle barns are empty, yet you should rejoice in Me! Be joyful in Me, the God of your salvation!*
>*- Habakkuk 3:17-18 (NLT)*

I need Your help Lord. I will, yes, praise You no matter what. But I need Your help. I have no fancy words or supplications, I just simply need Your help.

>*I will make rivers in the dry wasteland so that you, My chosen, can be refreshed. - Isaiah 43:20 (NLT)*

I will hold You to Your Word Lord God. You sound so real to me now. I will hold You to Your Word.

>*You have received full payment and are amply supplied. - Philippians 4:18 (NIV)*

As scary as it sounds, I will choose to believe that, even before I see it. Even though I still have great need.

>*I Am your Shepherd; you have all that you need. - Psalm 23:1 (NLT)*

>*You will be blessed if you trust in Me. - Psalm 84:12 (NIV)*

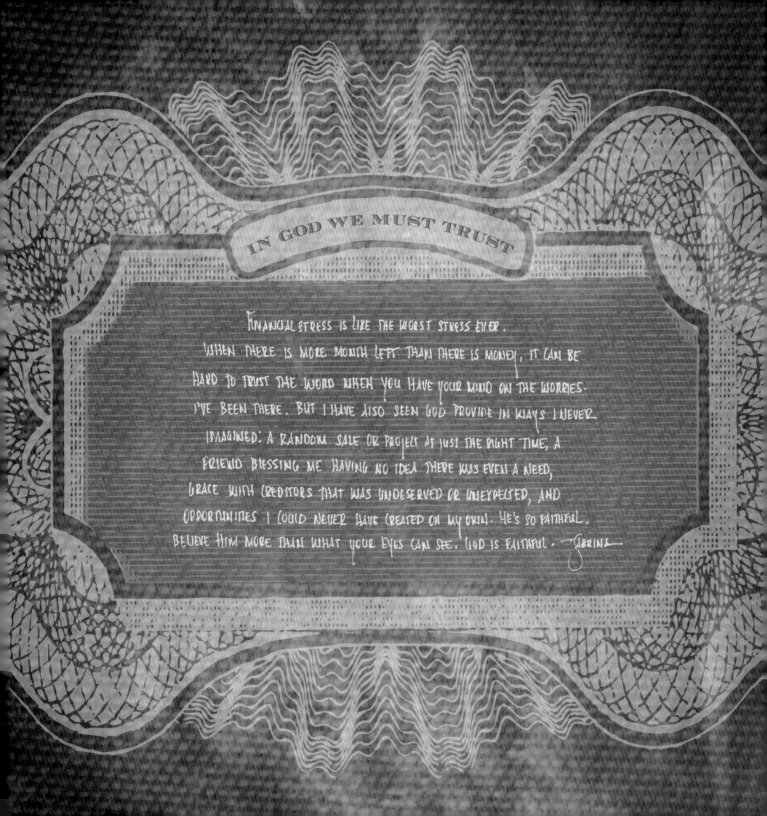

IN GOD WE MUST TRUST

Financial stress is like the worst stress ever.
When there is more month left than there is money, it can be
hard to trust the word when you have your mind on the worries.
I've been there. But I have also seen God provide in ways I never
imagined: a random sale or project at just the right time, a
friend blessing me having no idea there was even a need,
grace with creditors that was undeserved or unexpected, and
opportunities I could never have created on my own. He's so faithful.
Believe Him more than what your eyes can see. God is faithful. – Sabrina

before the last

This last chapter...the last chapter about waiting, is the hardest to write. It is the hardest to write because at the time of this writing, it is the season we are currently in. God has given our family a promise, a word, a HUGE covenant over our life together that goes against everything that we can physically see. Even as I type this, we are waiting.

Even as I type this, my spirit pleads with God to manifest His promise over our family. FINALLY.

It's one of the most painful processes ever.

To know, but have no idea. To foresee, but not know when. To do everything you know to do...

But yet you wait.

And wait.

And wait.

So every word that follows:

Every
Single
Word my friend...

We are currently still standing on. Clinging to. Holding God to. Crying out to Him.

Like literally crying. Waiting is the hardest thing ever.

So as you read, know that we feel you deeply if you are also in a season of waiting. I don't know you, but I am praying for you. If this season of waiting feels like it is tearing you apart little by little, but you refuse to let go of your promise, you are not alone, my friend.

You are not alone.

Now read on. And be encouraged.

His Word over each of us is true.
Even while we wait.

Pick up the phone Lord...
the waiting is too hard to endure

I know what You told me. All the Scripture I've gotten and every devotional I've read points to the same thing. Father please. How much longer must I wait?

If you look forward to something you don't yet have, you must wait patiently and confidently. - Romans 8:25 (NLT)

Patience. The dreaded P-word. I think I went to the bathroom when you handed out that fruit of the Spirit. I'm dying here Lord. Suspense is not one of my favorite things! What am I supposed to do with all of this waiting?

Be still and wait patiently for Me to act. - Psalm 37:7 (NIRV)

That's your answer for what I'm supposed to do? Wait some more? I've been standing on these promises for what seems like years now! Can you understand how awful it is to just wait and wait some more? Why show me so long ago if it would take so long? That's torture! That feels so mean to me! And I know You are not mean!

The message I give you waits for the time I have appointed. It speaks about what is going to happen. And all of it will come true. It might take awhile. But wait for it. You can be sure it will come. It will happen when I want it to.
- Habakkuk 2:3 (NIRV)

In all seriousness, I am struggling in my waiting. Father I am trying to keep the faith. But with every day that goes past, my anxiety heightens over if I heard You right and if it will ever happen. Lord, please help me in this waiting. I think it is really chipping away at my very soul.

Don't let your heart be troubled. Trust in Me. When everything is ready, I will come and get you. - John 14:1-3 (NLT)

Why tell me at all? Now I tick days down to what I cannot know is the final day. Each day just goes by with nothing. Why tell me? Why show me at all? Why not just make it happen and surprise me when it was actually time? I don't understand why You would do that?

I have told you these things before they happen so that when they do happen, you will believe. - John 14:29 (NLT)

Have you changed your mind? Am I holding on and waiting for nothing?

No, I will not break My covenant; I will not take back a single word I said. - Psalm 89:34 (NLT)

It's so humbling because I'm waiting, my family is waiting, and I've even gotten close friends involved. We are all looking for something that I am not entirely sure is even going to actually happen anymore. I'm so afraid and this constant waiting, day after day, is not helping me.

Write this down, for what I tell you is trustworthy and true. - Revelation 21:5 (NLT)

I Am not a man, so I do not lie. I Am not human, so I do not change My mind. Have I ever spoken and failed to act? Have I ever promised and not carried it through? - Numbers 23:19 (NLT)

If I said it, I will do it! - 1 Thessalonians 5:24 (MSG)

Not a single one of all the good promises that I have given is left unfulfilled; everything I have spoken comes true. - Joshua 21:45 (NLT)

I don't see any sign of things actually happening. Can I at least have a sign? An assurance that things are actually moving and aligning? Lord please! This waiting!

Live by believing and not by seeing. - 2 Corinthians 5:7 (NIRV)

So You are doing things for me? That I cannot see? Things that line up to what You have shown me? Things that support what I am waiting on and praying so hard about?

Since the world began, no ear has heard and no eye has seen a God like Me, who works for those who wait for Me! - Isaiah 64:4 (NLT)

Lord. Waiting is the worst thing ever. I am just trying to trust You in this process. I just get so afraid that You have changed Your mind or that I've done something to mess it all up. It's terrifying to think that I am holding on for something that will no longer be happening for me. Is that horrible? Do I sound like I'm losing faith? I hope not. I am just so tired of waiting. I'm doing everything I know to do to bide my time. It's just so hard.

I, the Lord of Heaven's Armies have spoken- who can change My plans? When my hand is raised, who can stop Me?
- Isaiah 14:27 (NLT)

I, the Lord of Heaven's Armies have sworn this oath: "It will all happen as I have planned. It will be as I have decided."
- Isaiah 14:24 (NLT)

Understand, therefore, that I, the Lord your God, am indeed God. I am the faithful God who keeps My covenant for a thousand generations and lavishes My unfailing love on those who love Me and obey My commands. - Deuteronomy 7:9 (NLT)

I remind myself of my kids. I know what I told them and yet they still question me. What am I doing? I'm sorry Lord. I will take You at every Word. When I feel weak, or frustrated, or nervous about Your promise to me, please just send me Your Word and Your assurance. But for now, You have shown Yourself clear: My promise still stands. If I will only trust You, keep my eyes on You, and wait. Through tears and all, I will wait.

You are blessed because you believed that I would do what I said. - Luke 1:45 (NLT)

I will keep you in perfect peace when you keep your mind on Me. If you will just trust Me.

- Isaiah 26:3

THE LORD

WHO CAN STOP ME

I, THE LORD OF HEAVEN'S ARMIES HAVE SPOKEN - WHO CAN CHANGE MY PLANS?
WHEN MY HAND IS RAISED, WHO CAN STOP ME?

ISAIAH 14:27

epilogue

Writing this book was an experience by itself.

I know I told you at the beginning of this book that my manuscript was already in place, through the pages of a completed journal.

It should have been as simple as copy, paste, edit, submit, right?

WRONG. Couldn't have been any more wrong.

I went through long bouts of distraction, disobedience, and downright rebellion. BUT AGAIN, He met me at every single turn:

Do you remember that scene in the film The Color Purple, when Whoopi Goldberg's character puts the mojo on Danny Glover with the line, "Until you do right by me? Everything you even think about is gonna fail?" Well I know God doesn't put mojos on people, but I'm pretty sure He slammed fast quite a few doors while I was in my moments of disobedience.

Literally, my other endeavors came to a screeching halt. New ideas that I tried to implement when I knew I should have been writing fell apart before my very eyes. Friends I longed to see and spend fun time with instead of dedicating time to my writing were no longer as available as they had been. I even grew to dislike social media (Wait, What?? Me disliking Facebook???) Yes! Absolutely, because God placed a hardening of my heart in that area. He knew it was a major time sucker and distraction.

Until I did right by what HE told me to do, everything I even thought about failed.

But the opposite was also true.

When I focused on this book, things happened. Business picked up in my other ventures, friends texted and replied to my texts, and ideas flowed like water. It was near immediate! I would sit down to type, and orders would start coming into the Shop. New contracts and projects would show up for my husband when he began to be obedient in his commitment to illustrate. And it just felt BETTER.

This does not even account for all of the WORD I received during this writing period on obedience. God beat me over the head with it.

But not really.

He never beats us over the head with anything. But He does love us too much to let us go. He loved us too much to allow us to miss the blessing that is The Red Phone Chronicles. He loved us too much to allow us to be disobedient.

If it meant shutting things off until we got it.
If it meant shutting things on so we could see it.
If it meant filling our ears with Scripture on obedience and the price of disobedience.
If it meant using random people who had NO IDEA I WAS WRITING A BOOK to say things like:

- Hey you should write a book!
- Everyone has a story to tell. Go tell it before it's too late.
  (This was a perfect stranger. Crazy!)
- Whatever God has for you, it's big. You'd better listen.
- I feel like God is telling you to scream your faith.

If it meant the difference between us obeying and writing this book, or us being disobedient and missing this charge (and blessing!) He was willing to do anything.

And I love Him for that.

Read this book with great care. If you see yourself in our cries, our pains, our anger, our frustration, in any of it, know that you are not alone. But I say to you again:

He's got a Word for all of it.

Read it as many times as you need to. Seek the Scriptures out in their entirety for yourself. Share them with friends who need them. But most of all, pray. And listen.

He's ready and waiting to pick up your Red Phone calls.

I know because He answered mine. And He still does.

He always will.

acknowledgments

First and foremost, none of this would be here without my God. Tearing up at the thought of Him, I realize and understand that to hear Him with such clarity is a gift. I acknowledge, honor, and thank Him indeed for giving me ears to hear and eyes to see Him. Thank You Jesus for loving me too much to let me miss. Thank You for making that gift available to all who are willing.

My husband Chris and my girls. Our family has gone through the ringer, down the road, up the alley, and back again. But through it all we have shone with a Light brighter than I could ever imagine. That's Jesus. He has that effect, even on a family that is going through, if we will let Him. I love you guys so much.

My Mom & Bigmama. Paying homage to the days when there was no such thing as kids with a choice of whether they could go to church or not. Thank you for raising me up in the way that I should go. I did not, and never will, depart from it.

My ladies-in-prayer, my Aarons and my Urs, my armor-bearers, my affectionately-coined #RideorDie girls who prayed me through this process, let me sob it out on the phone, via text, FaceTime, or on their person. My absolute dearest friends and sisters: Sharon, Pamela, Alycia, Christine, Michelle, Felicia, Cherise, Neodesha, Aileen, Martine, Natasha, Abi, Mama Angie, Sabrina on the rooftop in Haiti, my and beautifully aware Ingrid with the rainbows. I just have no words. Your love and friendship, discernment of me in the Spirit, intercessory prayer, and God's provision in you just cannot be described. I love you. That's all I got.

My amazing friend, sister-of-the-cloth, and editor, Dr. Sandi Arroyo. You mean so much to me and I am so proud of you. Thank you.

To our Church at Chapel Hill family, particularly Pastor Dave & Cindy Divine and Pastor Jamal Baker, your hand of blessing upon our family and ministry will never be forgotten. Thank you for filling up hospital waiting rooms to the dismay of staff but for the honor of our Lord. We love you all so much and after 12 years, there is nowhere else we'd rather be.

All of the women who participate in Sanctuary Girl! Thank you for cheering me on and not letting me succumb to my fears! I love you so much!

If you feel as if you were forgotten, you are not forgotten. There are so many who show such boundless support and I am ever thankful. Please know that you hold my heart. I love you.

thank you

Thank you for reading!

Stay the course and keep your head up.

God's got us.

And He's got you!

Love Always in Christ,

The Hayeses

discussion guide

Red Phone Chronicles: Pick Up the Phone Lord, It's an Emergency

Red Phone Chronicles covers a lot. From anger to anxiety, failure to fear, and discouragement to disobedience, everything any of us could possibly experience while doing this thing called life is in the pages of this book.

While God responds to us directly, tangibly, and with clarity through His Word, sometimes it is good to dig a little deeper; to ask yourself the hard questions about your own specific situation.

Take your time through the questions. Really think about them. Write your thoughts in a journal, meditate on your answers, and allow God to minister to you as you dive deeper.

Gather a few trusted friends, your small group or book club, your journal and pen, and let's begin.

Pick up the phone Lord! I feel like a failure.

Let's talk about it.

Could you relate to this chapter? In what area of your life, personally, spiritually, or even professionally, are you experiencing feelings of failure?

In Red Phone, one of my cries is that I've tried everything. God's response is essentially to try HIM. Stop for a moment and consider, have you been operating in your own solutions, your own logic, or even your own strength in order to succeed? How do you know when you've fallen into this trap?

Do you believe your feelings of failure interfere with your ability to hear from God? Do you believe your feelings of failure have affected your level of faith? In what ways?

God responds to my expression of fatigue in trying by acknowledging that He has been watching me attempt, and watching me fail. Do you think that God allows us to fail, knowing that at any time He can open the door or provide the answers we need? If so, why do you think He allows this?

One of the most popular Scriptures can be found in this dialogue: All things work together for your good. How has God used prior failures in your life for your good? When you examine your life in retrospect, how can you see where a moment or even a season of failures actually worked out for you? Does that encourage you in your present moment of failure?

God says not to rely on your own understanding. What are some practical and tangible ways that you can be sure you are not relying on your own brains or brawn to succeed? How can you be sure that you are relying on Him first and not yourself?

The Lord talks about total commitment. Think about the area in which you are feeling feelings of failure. Can you honestly lay your work before the Lord and say that you have been totally committed? When you examine yourself, your efforts, and even your time spent in prayer, have you fully committed yourself to your goal? Or have there been real gaps in your focus? Explore this topic and take your time. I found that when I held my own feet to the fire in accountability, that my feelings of failure were being fed by deficiencies in my own behavior. Addressing these deficiencies (waking earlier to have more time to work, calendar blocking, limiting distractions in my day, seeking wisdom, etc.) helped me to succeed. Where do you see areas of improvement for yourself that can be coupled with relying more on God?

When we put God first, failure doesn't feel so bad. When we know that we are doing what we are doing with the audience of One in mind, failure doesn't feel so bad. Write down your areas of failure and ask God to reveal to you where you've been operating in your own strength and forgetting to put Him first, where you need His help to be fully committed, and lastly, for new and fresh wisdom on how to pick up and start again. Watch for His responses and write them down! He is faithful!

Pick up the phone Lord! I don't know what to do.

Let's discuss.

Could you relate to this chapter? Have you ever reached the end of yourself and had no idea what to do or what would happen next? Describe it and how it made you feel.

'Be still, and know that I am God.' What do you think God means by this? How does this compare to the natural ways we tend to react when we don't know what to do? Do you think this verse is unreasonable?

God reminds me several times that He is directing my steps, and that His ways are higher than mine. Can you recount a time or season in your life when answers or next steps came to you in such a way that you knew they were from God Himself?

What are some practical ways that we can seek God first even in the midst of being frustrated with the lack of answers or direction? Include in this ways we can manage the stress of not knowing, even when it seems unmanageable.

Do you think it is sinful to be frustrated with not knowing what's next? If so, why? If not, when does it actually lead to sin?

Break down the passage located in Psalm 105:1-6. Rate yourself on how much time you spend giving thanks, proclaiming how good God is (even when things don't seem so good!), exulting in His Name, seeking Him out, and reflecting on how He has come through for you before. Spend time asking Him to help you increase where you need to, putting Him ahead of the need to know, and learning to trust Him more. He will help you!

Pick up the phone Lord! I'm so angry and cannot forgive.

This is a good one. Lets dig in.

Hard question number one: Is it okay to be deeply offended? Before we even graduate to not forgiving, how do you think God feels about us feeling angry, offended, or extremely disappointed in someone?

Are there any offenses that you believe God would be okay with you taking the posture of not being willing to forgive? Have you experienced a hurt that you believe God is okay with you not forgiving, or even taking your time in deciding if you want to forgive or not?

Do you think it's unreasonable for God to expect us to forgive others like He forgives us? He is God after all, and we are not… right? Is it possible for us to forgive like He does? Realistically? Ponder that question and answer honestly.

How does it make you feel to hear God say, "I do not treat you as your sins deserve or repay you according to your iniquities?"

Real talk moment: If you have to stand before God tomorrow, unexpectedly, and the measure of forgiveness and grace that you are given directly reflects the measure of forgiveness and grace that you were willing to give while you were here, would it bode well for you? Or would you be in trouble? How does that make you feel about your attitudes today?

What does Scripture tell us to do when we are having a hard time forgiving and getting past anger? What are some practical ways we can work through forgiving the unforgivable?

Meditation moment: Think about a few times where you know that you have deeply offended, disappointed, or even angered God. Consider what He says in Psalm 103:12 in relation to those moments of failure. Then take your journal and write down three situations or people where you know you have struggled to completely forgive. Pray and ask God to help you. He will.

Pick up the phone Lord! Everyone hates me, and I think it's all Your fault.

Are you ready?

Did this chapter ping you at all? Have you had moments where you felt isolated and alone, or even as if no one liked you?

Do you think it is possible to serve for God, and not for people? Do you think it's possible to keep working and living for others without human reward or recognition? What makes it difficult? What does God expect of us according to His Word?

Meditation moment: Think about Isaiah 53:3. How does it make you feel?

What are some practical ways that we can work through being disliked or rejected because of our faith?

How does it make you feel to know that God is on your side, even when it feels like no one else is? Does it comfort you? Or do you still feel alone?

Study time: Where do we see two people in the Bible who feel like this? How did they respond? How do you relate to them? Does it help you to see that this is not as abnormal as it might feel and that it's not just you?

Pull out your journal and write about a time when you felt alone, ridiculed, judged, or even hated for your faith. In your prayer, ask God to help you to see those people through His eyes, loving them with His grace and forgiving them. Ask Him to send you like-minded friends to do your faith-life with and to share your journey. He is faithful!

Pick up the phone Lord! I'm down and can't pick myself up.

Get up. Let's get started.

If your heart is beating while you're reading this, then you can most likely relate to this section. Discuss, as you feel comfortable, a time when the sadness or the discouragement seemed to be more than you could bear. How did you get through it?

How does it make you feel to read 2 Corinthians 1:3-5, when God expresses an understanding of how you are feeling? What do you think of His explanation of why you may be feeling at your lowest? Do you think that this is a lesson you have personally learned through your experience of feeling down?

God calls Himself the "Father of mercies" and the "God of all comfort." What are some ways that we can tangibly feel and experience His mercy and comfort when we are feeling bad?

Philippians 4:8 gives us a long list of things to think about when our minds start to journey to dark places. In your journal, in one column, make a list of the six things that this passage of Scripture tells you to focus on (true, noble, right, lovely, admirable, excellent or praiseworthy.) Next to each category, list or describe something or someone that fits. Give yourself some practice on training your mind to think on good things, even when circumstances try to have you focus on the negative.

What do you think God is trying to tell you in Matthew 5:14-16? Why is it ultimately important that we don't stay down for long?

Pick up the phone Lord! I'm a horrible parent.

This one is really an eye-opener. Let's begin.

I think you'd be hard-pressed to find a mom or dad who hasn't felt this way. As you are comfortable, discuss a parenting moment where you felt like you dropped the ball and failed miserably.

How do you know when you've run out of parenting steam? How does it manifest tangibly for you in your home and relationships with your kids?

What is God's response to the declaration that you just can't do it anymore? How does it make you feel to hear Him say that you should give it all you have because you are willing, and not just because you must?

Read John 3:30. What does it look like for God to become greater and for us to become less when it comes to parenting?

Meditation moment: Weigh your relationship with your kids, the easy times and the difficult times, against your own Parent-child relationship with God your Father. Where do you see striking similarities (e.g., not spending enough time with Him, but still asking for lots of things perhaps like teens tend to do!) or shocking differences (e.g., holding our kids offenses against them when they are going through long seasons of belligerence instead of forgiving them.) Seeing ourselves through God's eyes can really open our own eyes and reveal some much-needed details about our parenting. It can help us to parent from a God-perspective and less from a flesh-perspective! Discuss your findings.

What are some practical ways you can train your kids up as Scripture instructs us to?

What are some practical ways we can make it through difficult parenting moments according to Scripture? Write these down! You'll most likely need them later!

Pick up the phone Lord! I feel so alone.

Take your time with this one. Let's dig in.

Could you relate to the feelings of loneliness in this section? How do you think it's possible for someone to feel lonely even when they are surrounded by or have access to friends and family?

Do you think it's possible that God allows us to experience solitude or loneliness in order to draw us closer to Him?

Why do you think it's so difficult to share our feelings of loneliness with others or even with God Himself?

Read Isaiah 49:15-16. Then read it again. Close your eyes and let the last sentence sink in: See I have written your name on the palms of My hands. Do you see the correlation between your importance and Jesus' sacrifice? Meditate on the hidden treasure in this verse. How does it make you feel to know you are so important to Him that you are forever engraved on the palm of His hands by nails driven at the cross? How does it line up with the thoughts you may have about being lonely or forgotten?

What things or conditions cause people to think that they are separated from God's love? How does Romans 8:38 answer this question?

Study Time! Discuss two situations where God's Presence showed up for someone in the Bible who was in a moment of solitude. Do you see yourself in any of these scenarios?

What are some ways that we can make it through our lonely spells, both Scriptural and practical? Write these down in your journal and remember to draw on these when you feel alone.

Pick up the phone Lord! I want to try but I'm afraid of rejection.

It can be daunting to talk about, but let's get started.
I think there is a point in everyone's life where they will experience rejection. Discuss one memorable time or season where the fear of rejection kept you from wanting to even make an attempt to step out in faith.

God describes those whose opinions we fear as "mere humans" in Isaiah 51. Why do you think we have such fear of the rejection of "mere humans" even when we know they cannot really do anything to us?

Do you think pride has anything to do with our fear of rejection and its leading to our inability to obey? Would you surmise that fear of rejection is actually sinful behavior?

How does it make you feel to know that when God has called you to do something, that it is a "fearful responsibility" to Him? Does it put your hesitation to act in a more serious light?

What does God promise us if we commit our work to Him? What does He provide for us in His Word if we do all things for Him and not just for man, even when we are afraid?

Study time: Locate one person in the Bible who struggled with the thought of rejection. What was their dilemma and how did they handle it?

What are three practical ways you can press through the fear of rejection? Using your journal, form affirmations for yourself using three Scriptures to counter fearful thoughts that may arise when you worry about rejection. Pray them over yourself when you feel nervous about stepping out on faith to complete an assignment you've been given.

Pick up the phone Lord! I need a do-over.

Ready? Let's go.

Describe one moment where you felt like if you were given another opportunity to do it over, and to do it RIGHT, you would have given anything for the chance.

How can God use even our mess-ups for our good? Can you think of specific examples?

The Lord describes us as having a "stony, stubborn heart." Is it sobering to realize that when we refuse to give Him even the mess we've made in exchange for His "new" that we are actually being stubborn? How does God respond to our stubbornness?

Why can it be so difficult to believe that God doesn't hold our mess against us?

If the area in which you need a do-over is relational, give some thought to how you can initiate a fresh start. What are some practical ways that you can restore or refresh a strained relationship in your life?

If the area in which you need a do-over is financial or professional, give some thought to how you can begin again. What are some practical ways that you can press the reset button on your finances or your career?

Letting go. It can be difficult. Using your journal, privately put the mess you've made down on paper. Repent of any behavior that may have caused the mess and leave it behind. Pray Ezekiel 36:26-27 over yourself. Memorize it and accept the tender and responsive heart that God has for you! It's your time to begin again!

Pick up the phone Lord! My anxiety is going to kill me.

I think this is one of my favorites. Let's dig in.

Anxiety. You can't be a living and breathing thing if you have not experienced anxiety or stress at some point. Discuss, as you are comfortable, an area where you struggle with anxiety or high levels of stress in your life.

Do you think it's reasonable for God to ask us not to worry about details and to only focus on Him? Or is He asking too much? Is it possible for humans NOT to stress over things?

God calls us out about whether or not worrying adds to our life. In actuality, worrying can take away from our lives! What are some real life ways that anxiety and stress affect us negatively? Include effects on our bodies, our minds, and even on those around us.

What do we learn about giving our cares and worries to God instead of retaining them? What does that process look like in real life?

Be still. How difficult is it to hear that phrase when there is so much going on and the last thing you feel like you can afford to do is to be still? Why do you think God compels us to do something that is against our very nature when it comes to worry and anxiety?

God says that He will never fail us or abandon us. Many times, it helps to meditate on past situations where God did indeed show HImself faithful in order to keep ourselves encouraged in stressful moments. Using your journal, take some time to think back to high-anxiety or stressful moments where God delivered you, provided you with assurance or peace, or even divine solutions.

God provides us with a gift of peace of mind and heart according to His Word. What are some spiritual, emotional, and even tangible ways that we can activate this peace within our hearts and not succumb to anxiety. Write these down and train your mind to use these tools when you feel anxiety coming on!

Pick up the phone Lord! No one is supporting me.

It's sad to talk about, but let's do it anyway. Here we go.

Have you ever put your heart into something only to have it be met with lackluster response?

Discuss the situation, as you are comfortable, and how it made you feel.

What do you think it means to be okay with working for an audience of One?

How does it make you feel to think on the fact that not only does God understand how you feel when people ignore and reject you, but that He experienced it Himself?

God compels us to humble ourselves before Him in order to then be lifted up. What do you think "humbling yourself" looks like in your life and in your efforts?

It hurts when we don't get the response or the support we'd like to get from people. How can we "work for God rather than for people?" How can we protect ourselves from the feelings of resentment or bitterness that can rise up when we feel unsupported in our efforts? How can we ensure that we are working more for God's approval than for man?

Do you think there are areas where you have allowed pride to seep in to your efforts, thus creating the need for man's approval instead of God's approval? Discuss as you are comfortable.

Using your journal, commit what you are doing to paper. Find a prayer and accountability partner and agree with them in prayer for God's approval and success in your efforts. He is faithful!

Pick up the phone Lord! I can't hear You.

Let's talk this through.

Have you experienced a moment, a time, or a season where you felt like you weren't hearing from God? Discuss, as you are comfortable, the scenario and how it made you feel.

How do you know when you are hearing from God versus when you are not?

Do you think that there are indeed moments where God intentionally goes silent? Do you think that there are distractions or obstacles in the way of us hearing from God?

There are many voices that fill our ears, particularly four: those of the people around us, our own, God, and even our enemy, Satan. Discuss the qualities of and how we can recognize each of these. Talk about which we should listen to and how to decide if we should act on what we hear from them.

Is it possible in some moments that we actually are hearing from God, but we are choosing not to listen, or to ultimately obey? Discuss, as you are comfortable, a time when you knew this was the case for you.

I compare God's communication with me to that of Noah, Solomon, and Abraham. What is so amazing about how God spoke to them? Do you think it is still possible for us to hear Him as clearly as they did?

God compels us in His Word to "let His Words penetrate deep into our hearts." What are some tangible ways that we can accomplish this command?

Using your journal, write a letter to the Lord telling Him that you want to hear from Him. Commit to Him your willingness to seek His voice in Scripture, to honor Him by being open to listen and to obey, and to commit His Word to memory. Write down any obstacles or distractions that may be prohibiting you from hearing Him and make a plan to minimize or even eliminate them. Determine to hear Him no matter what it takes!

Pick up the phone Lord! I don't even know why I'm here.

This section can be painful. It's hard to think we have no purpose. Let's talk it through.

Comparison is a doozy. Discuss, as you are comfortable, a struggle you have with comparing your life, purpose, or even meaning, to others that you see. Talk about how and why we feel compelled to compare and the effect that it can have on us.

Knowing that you were specifically handcrafted by God, does it make sense that with the creation of your body, that He also designed you a certain way for a certain purpose? He calls us His "masterpiece." Discuss what you believe makes you different, what makes you a piece of art, and where you feel these characteristics make you most purposeful.

God says that you are chosen, but chosen for what? What is your ultimate purpose here on the earth as a Child of God according to Scripture? Talk about how it makes you feel to hear His Words: "You didn't choose Me. I chose you."

When we yield ourselves to God's purpose and will for our lives, what does He promise us?

He tells us that His gifts can not be withdrawn. Do you know what your gifts are? Find a Holy Spirit Gifts test online or through your local church and administer it to yourself. Do these gifts line up with your natural talents and passions? I think you'll be surprised!

Agree in prayer with your group that God would begin to develop your purposes, cultivate your gifts, and reveal your mission to you. Hold each other accountable in seeking God's will, ask Him to make clear the paths that you should take, and to increase your opportunities to do His work that He planned for you to do long ago. He is faithful!

Pick up the phone Lord! I'm trying so hard to live right, but I'm struggling.

Okay! This section can be a bit challenging, but let's get 'er done!

Can we be very transparent here? Are there times when we as Christians feel that others have more freedom to do what they will, when they will, how they will? What activities do you see that sometimes, even in the smallest way, you wish you could participate in without feeling bad about it? Discuss as you are comfortable.

What is the difference between being dominated by the Spirit versus being dominated by the sinful nature? How can you tangibly tell which one is at work in you in any given moment?

What does Scripture say is the striking difference between those who have the Spirit living in them and those who do not? Where does the Word say that letting the sinful nature control us will lead?

The Word says that there are penalties to letting our sinful nature control us, even upon our own homes. Discuss possible consequences to ourselves, our families, or even the generations after us if we succumb to our flesh desires to sin. Provide real-life examples, as you are comfortable.

God gives us a bit of real talk in Scripture by saying we are liars if we profess Him, but continue to live in spiritual darkness. How does that make the question of purposely leaning just a little bit towards sin even more serious?

Satan will tempt us in ways that diminish the seriousness of sin by enticing us with its benefits, belittling its impact on our lives, or even attempting to convince us that it isn't sin at all. How does Scripture tell us and equip us to negate these tactics?

Being good or perfect won't save us. That has been accomplished by the power of the Cross. But ultimately, why should we do our best, in every way, to still live a life that is holy and pleasing to the Lord?

Using your journal, consider areas of sin weakness in your life. Write them down and ask God to make you new in these areas, helping you to lead a life that is good and holy. If comfortable, share them with an accountability partner who can help you to seek God and stay strong in these areas for help.

Pick up the Phone Lord! My faith is on its way out.

Have faith. Two of the most profound, yet torturous words ever. Let's discuss.

Discuss something you've been "faithing" it on. As you are comfortable, discuss one thing that you've been standing on, praying for, and trusting God for over time. Where are you in your faith process? Seeing progress or still waiting?

I express a bit of frustration with God in our dialogue. He states His case that He takes care of everything else in the world, including flowers, so I should trust that He will take care of me. Do you think it is unfair of God to chastise our faith as small knowing how difficult it can be to withstand what we see in real life? Do we have a right to be frustrated? Do we have a right to want a break from "faith standing" sometimes?

God's Word to us is very sobering. What does He say about people who run after worries such as those we carry? How does this make you feel? What is His instruction for us when it comes to worrying?

What does God tell us to do when we know the Word, yet we grow weak in standing on the Word regarding our promises? What are some tangible ways we can accomplish this and stay strong in our faith and trust in God?

What is important to know about how doubt plays into standing on faith? What things can seep in and sow seeds of doubt?

God asks us to think on if He has ever promised and not seen us through. Remembering past seasons when we stood on faith to the end and He showed up for us can help us get through future long seasons of faith. Recount a time when you stood on faith for something or someone, and God answered you. Remember these moments when it gets hard. If He did it before, He will do it again. Stay the course my friends and don't give up.

Pick up the phone Lord! I feel so unloved.

Feeling unloved is one of the hardest things ever. Let's talk about it.

Could you relate in any way to this section? Have you experienced a time when you felt unloved? Discuss as you are comfortable.

God tells us that He has written us on the palms of His hands. Discuss the meaning of this verse and how it really makes you feel when it comes to feeling loved.

What causes us as humans to often feel unloved? Where do we suffer the neglect or lack of relationship that can lead to this feeling? Is it possible that sometimes we convince ourselves that we are unloved, even when we know that this is not true?

Meditation moment: Among all the billions of souls on earth, according to His Word, He sees you and He knows you by name. You are precious to Him. You are honored. He loves you. Meditate in that warmth for a moment. How does that make you feel to know that you are so loved by God, even if you feel so unloved by humans?

Once you know and understand even a fraction of how much God loves you, it becomes more difficult to hold others' love for you to such a high standard. How does God compare how He loves you to how people may love you? What sets His great love for you apart from anyone else?

Quiet time: Put everything down, lay back, and just bask in the light and warmth that is the love of God for you. Talk with Him about how you are feeling and ask Him to pour out His immeasurable love and grace over you, to wash away any feelings of sadness or loneliness, and to fill you with his joy and grace. Ask Him to show Himself to you through others who also love Him and to grant you fellowship with the body through the spirit of oneness and mutual affection. He is faithful. You are loved. He cares for you too much to let you feel otherwise.

Pick up the phone Lord! I feel like I'm drowning and I'm so overwhelmed.

Snap on your life jacket and let's talk through it!

Raise your hand if you're overwhelmed! I can imagine all of the hands that went up. It's very common for us to have way too much on a plate that's entirely too small, and I'm not talking cake! Discuss, as you are comfortable, an area where you feel utterly overwhelmed.

What are your normal go-tos when you are feeling this way? What are your usual ways of managing high levels of stress, anxiety, and a neverending to-do list? How do these methods differ from what Scripture compels us to do when we feel like we are distressed?

In 2 Corinthians 8:9-10, God actually acknowledges and validates how we are feeling! He not only restates our feelings, but He actually tells us to recognize the lesson in them. What is the lesson to be learned in feeling overwhelmed according to this Scripture?

The Lord has an "I told you so" moment in Matthew 6. What does He warn us against in this passage? How do we know that worrying actually has a negative effect on us, both physically and emotionally?

What do you think God means when He tells us to find joy in His commands, even when we are facing pressure and stress? How do you think that can help us in our times of strain?

What are some tangible ways that we can truly give our burdens over to God? How can we practice keeping our thoughts on Him, even when we are under great pressure?

What two things does God promise us in return for our endurance through suffering and trials? Also, why does He say that it is important that we persevere through these moments when it comes to our witness?

Using your journal, make a list of the top three things that have you feeling inundated with stress and tension. Ask God to grant you wisdom on how best to deal with these things, to give you peace in the process, and provision to walk through them with Him. He is faithful to perform His Word when we trust Him!

Pick up the phone Lord! My enemies are attacking me.

Oh boy. Put down the boxing gloves for a minute, and let's talk it out. Here we go.

Offenses against us happen everywhere: in our homes, places of work, friendships, marriages, and even church and on social media. Discuss, as you are a comfortable, an area where you can sense someone is offending or attacking you on purpose.

How does our human side naturally react to being attacked or offended? Why do you think it is so easy to fall into reacting this way?

Meditation moment: Our model for everything we do is Jesus. Discuss moments in Scripture when He was attacked. What were some of His responses to these offenses against Him? How do His reactions compare to our own?

Why does God tell us that it is important that we conduct ourselves with integrity before others, even when we are under attack? Do you think it is a reflection of our character and our faith if we react in the wrong way before others, even in the name of self-defense?

I told God that He was asking a lot for me to behave in the face of attack. What was His response? When you stop to think about Jesus and His experience, does it still seem like God is asking a lot of us? Does it help you to want to react differently when under attack when you think about how much Jesus went through, yet He still maintained a holy posture of grace and forgiveness?

The Lord doesn't discount the real fact that we have enemies. How does He assure us that as we seek to model Him, that He will indeed take care of THEM? What does He promise us in His Word regarding taking up our defense? How does this make you feel?

When we take advantage of God's offer to defend us while we turn our focus to Him instead of our enemies, we become less susceptible to offense. Using your journal, make a short list of three people that you know are either attacking you or view you as their enemy. In prayer, ask God to see to them as you turn your focus to Him. Ask Him to show you any areas of sin or offense towards them that may reside in your own heart, and to replace them with a heart of repentance, forgiveness, and grace. Do the BIG thing, if you are able, and pray the same prayer over them. God can turn hearts around faster than our retaliation ever can!

DISCLAIMER: If someone is attacking you in an abusive manner, seek help. God wants to help us, but He also expects us to operate with wisdom. If you are being abused, get out, and seek help immediately. Abuse in any form is not okay.

Pick up the phone Lord! I've sinned and I feel so ashamed.

Let's begin.

We know when we are wrong. Deep down we know. Discuss, as you are comfortable, a time when you knew you were wrong and you felt bad about it.

What are three sources of condemnation over us when it comes to sin? How do these messages compare to what God says about those of us who belong to Jesus?

How do we recognize shame and guilt in ourselves when it comes to sin? What are signs, including physical, spiritual, and emotional, that we are living under a heavy mantle of condemnation instead of grace?

What is God's clear Word for us regarding condemnation? What does He say He has done with our sins after we accept Jesus Christ's sacrifice for us? What is His response to us now through the lens of the Cross?

Meditation moment: You sinned. You will sin again. And again. And again. And probably a few more times after that. I think you understand that it will be impossible for us to lead a sin-free life! Viewing yourself through God's eyes in light of the Cross, what is now your understanding about how God sees you, even with your sinful nature?

Study time: Knowing that by grace we are saved, even though we often fail, do you believe this gives us a free license to do whatever we want, even if it's sinful? Why or why not?

What should be your process when you are aware of sin in your life according to Scripture? What does it mean to repent? What does it mean to you to know that you have a clean slate?

Using your journal, have a private time of confession between you and the Lord. Write down any sin or behavior that has had you burdened with the weight of guilt and condemnation. Ask Him to give you a new heart in these areas and to help you to sin no more. Accept the forgiveness freely given you and walk into a fresh start, committing to honoring Him with your life moving forward. Repeat as needed, because you'll need to! But He is faithful. His love covers a multitude of our sin. He's so good to us.

DISCLAIMER: Part of the repentance process could be making things right with another if you have sinned against someone directly. Read Matthew 5:24. Be open to the Holy Spirit if He prompts you to make things right. Follow through even if it's hard. Your blessings could depend upon it.

Pick up the Phone Lord! Everyone else Is doing great but me.

Yikes. Yes this one is a toughie. Let's discuss.

Comparison is a doozy. If we are all transparent, we can probably come up with at least one example of how we fell victim to the green-eyed monster. Discuss, as you are comfortable, a time when you felt like an area in your life was not as good as someone else's.

Comparing ourselves to others can often be rooted in not being assured of who we are in ourselves. What does God say that you are in Ephesians 2? What does this passage remind us that God spoke over us, each of us, long ago?

Ephesians 3 reminds us that God does not think about us as we think about us. The things that we imagine over ourselves pale in comparison to what He is able to do through us. How does it make you feel to know that He is able to explode the possibilities in your own life far beyond what you envisioned?

Real talk time: If all of this is true for you, is it possible that all of this is also true for the people we compare ourselves to? Is it possible that the people we compare ourselves to are simply walking in the plans God has for them as we should be? How does it make you feel to think that instead of rejoicing in and activating the plans and purposes that God has for us, that we are spending more time watching the plans and purposes He has for someone else unfold? Discuss the downfalls behind spending our time and energy in this area instead of spending it where it belongs: walking in His perfect will for our own lives. What does it cost you in time, emotions, and even progress?

Why do you think God warns us against evaluating people by what they have or how they look? Especially given the digital age we live in, is it possible that we are comparing ourselves to something that may not even be authentic?

It can be a bitter pill to swallow to be reminded that Jesus Himself did not come to be served, or to garner public accolades, or to live a life that was better than everyone else's. What does God remind us to do in order to align our lives more with Christ's example? How can we avoid succumbing to the need to compare our lives to those of others?

Using your journal, share with God the areas of your life where you would like more of His divine purpose and push. Ask Him to use you mightily according to His plans for you and to help you to stay focused on Him, and less on them. He is faithful!

Pick up the phone Lord! I'm so discouraged.

I get it. Let's talk about it.

Could you relate to this conversation? Discuss, as you are comfortable, an area where you experienced, or are experiencing, discouragement.

What does our human side compel us to do when we are discouraged? What are our natural reactions to feeling as if nothing is working, moving forward, or happening for us?

God tells us that He will strengthen, help, and comfort us in times of dispiritedness. What are some tangible ways that we can grab ahold to this strength, help, and comfort?

When we are experiencing setbacks, obstacles, and frustrations, it can be easy to want to give up. How can we do what God asks of us in Isaiah 50:7: set our faces like stone and determine to do His will? How can we keep going even when it's hard? What are some physical, emotional, and spiritual ways that we can press through discouragement?

How does God shift our "focused on the now" perspective to an eternal one in 2 Corinthians 4? Why is it important to keep this in mind as we press through discouragement in our time here on earth?

Unbelief is a huge, almost overlooked sin. Is it possible that when we are severely discouraged, that we are actually placing more faith in what we can do rather than in what God is able to do? How can we avoid doing this?

Revelation 21:5 compels us to write down God's Word over us and to trust those Words. Using your journal, write down the areas of discouragement and unbelief in your life. Ask God to help you to incorporate more of Him and less of yourself into these areas. Ask Him to help you to commit them to Him and to help you keep going with your eyes on His great reward. Rise up renewed and ready to tackle these things knowing that He is with you.

Pick up the phone Lord! I feel unappreciated.

I've been here too. Let's chat it out.

Whether in parenting, marriage, work, friendship, or even ministry, there are moments when we can feel unappreciated. Discuss, as you are comfortable, a time or season when you felt undervalued.

Is it sobering to read in Matthew 20:28 that Jesus Himself did not come here looking for recognition or kudos for His work, but simply to serve others? How does that make you feel when measured against your own feelings of not being appreciated? Do you feel slightly chastised when God compels you to have the same attitude that Jesus has?

What encouragement does God give us in Galatians 6 when it comes to working hard for what seems to be little return or reward? Is it difficult in the day-to-day to stay Kingdom-minded in this area?

How does it make you feel to know that if no one else sees you, thanks you, or acknowledges your work and giving, that God sees you and all that you do? Does that help to alleviate your feelings?

God takes on the Father role heavily in Philippians 2. What does He warn us against pertaining to our attitudes when we are working or serving others? Can you take a look back at your reaction to unacknowledged efforts and see where you may have reacted with grumbling or complaining?

When every word we speak and every action we take is simply to honor and please God, our need for human acknowledgment and appreciation isn't as great. What are some tangible ways that we can make sure our efforts are committed to Him, seeking His approval only, and not that of man?

Why is it important that everyone sees that we are considerate in what we do? Is it possible that our responses to people in this area reflect badly on our life and witness as a Christian? Ultimately, who are we working and serving for? Can you commit your work to Him today for His approval, seeking Him first and only?

Pray today and thank God for being the God who sees you. Thank Him for seeing all that you do and ask Him to bless your efforts and cause them to succeed. Ask Him, according to His will, to reward you both here on earth and in heaven for all that you are doing for the Kingdom. He is faithful!

Pick up the phone Lord! My situation feels so hopeless.

This is a sad place to be. Let's talk it through.

Have you ever been here? Share, as you are comfortable.

Even for those of us who KNOW God's Word, hopeless seasons can make it difficult to stand on Scripture and believe. What do you do when you reach those moments of difficulty? When the lack of hope or solutions is too hard to simply have faith, even when you know that's ultimately exactly what you should do. How do you press through?

Think back on what seemed like an impossibly despondent situation. Did the circumstance resolve? Did you see God move? When you think back, how does the Word put forth in 2 Corinthians apply to where you've been?

What are some tangible ways that we can stay forward focused when our current situation weighs so heavily on us? How can we keep God's Word ahead of us when it seems as if everything else is failing?

Do you believe hopelessness is equal to unbelief or lack of faith? What is God's response to Abraham's show of faith despite what seemed like a huge reason not to believe? Do you see the blessing in having faith in God over what you can (or cannot) see?

Remembering who God is is a huge factor in maintaining our hope. He is the very God who created the universe, who gives us each breath that we breathe, and who raised Christ from the dead. Putting Him in His proper perspective can keep us focused on how much bigger God is than our problems. Who is God to you? Have you made him small? Using your journal, make a list of all that you know that He has done to help get yourself back into the proper perspective. He outweighs our problems and is the God of all hope. He can resurrect your situation and make all things new. You can trust Him with your life.

Pick up the phone Lord! I'm in so much pain.

This topic can hurt. Literally. But let's get to it.

Pain can come from many different sources: those we love, suffering loss, from words or actions that offend us, and even self-inflicted pain. Discuss, as you are comfortable, a memorable season of pain.

The Lord sympathizes with us by recognizing that pain can leave us broken and crushed. What are our normal methods for responding to or dealing with immense emotional pain in our lives?

In 2 Corinthians 4, God encourages us to remind us that we may have been hurt, but we are still standing. Remembering seasons of pain that we have gone through and come out the other side can help us when we enter new times of emotional struggle. Can you recount a time of great pain, that with God, time, and additional resources as needed, you made it through?

In moments of severe pain and hurt, many times our human nature is to withdraw from others, even those who wish to help. This can be a perfect time to draw closer to the Lord. What are some tangible ways that we can use our pain as a catalyst for increased intimacy in our relationship with God?

Loving us at our darkest means that God loves us when we are at our highest moments and our lowest. Does it bring you comfort to know that even when you are feeling low that God is there? Where do we find an example of Jesus Himself struggling through pain and turning to God for comfort? How can we follow in His example?

Many times God's comfort is given to us through others. What sources does He provide through other people that can help us navigate through painful seasons? Be open to how He provides what and who you need to heal. He is faithful if we are willing.

Pick up the phone Lord! I'm down to my very last.

Almost done! Let's dive in.

As you are comfortable, describe a time when you were fresh out of resources or even ideas on how to get the resources you needed.

What are our natural strategies as humans when we have reached the bottom of the financial bucket? How do these strategies compare to what God tells us to do in Matthew 6:33? Why is it easier to fall into trying to make things happen on our own rather than trusting God to provide?

We get what might seem to be unfathomable advice from Habakkuk 3 on how we should react even when our well has run dry. What do we find here? Do you think it is unreasonable of God to ask this of us when we are worried about something so big as having what we need to live and take care of our families?

Study time: Where do we find five passages in Scripture where God promises to provide for us? What are some practical ways that we can apply this Word and stand on these promises when we are struggling financially?

The Lord reminds us that we will be blessed if we trust in Him. What does that look like when provision appears to have run out? What does trusting Him more than you trust your bank balance look like in real life?

God's provision is more than just unexpected money. Discuss other ways we may have missed His provision and grace over us financially such as grace with creditors or keeping us safe from expensive harm. Talking these through can help us to see that He actually is working on our behalf!

Using your journal, have some private confession time with the Lord. Practice casting your anxiety in the area of provision on Him by writing down your needs. Ask Him to show Himself to you in this area and help you strengthen your faith. Ask Him to give you wisdom in your situation to know what to do according to His will. His word and His promise stands: He will never see the righteous forsaken. Stand on His promises today.

Pick up the phone Lord! The waiting is too hard to endure.

With every bone in my body I get it. Let's link arms and talk about waiting together.

Waiting. Let's talk about it. Who else is waiting? Offer your brief story as you are comfortable.

How many times does God compel us to wait, and to wait patiently? Does anyone else cringe at the word patient, or any derivative thereof? Do you think God understands how it can be difficult to be patient?

God asks us to "be still." Oftentimes in our waiting seasons, we try to make things happen on our time. Discuss how this can be detrimental to us, or even cause us more hardship than we would've experienced had we just waited and stayed still. Do you think this is wise advice from God?

What is God's answer in Habakkuk 2 and John 14:29 for why He makes us wait sometimes? Do you see how your waiting season can be a source of growth and refinement for you and your faith? Explain how this can happen as a result of waiting.

Trusting God during a waiting period, particularly a lengthy one, can be very difficult. What are some palpable ways that we can press through the waiting and keep frustration and discouragement at bay?

We explore at least three passages where God confirms and affirms Himself that when He says something, He means it. Read through these passages through the lens of being frustrated in waiting. Do you think it dishonors God when we are impatient or frustrated when things don't happen in our time, or if we even go so far as to doubt His Word in our waiting?

What we see with our physical eyes can contradict what our spiritual eyes fight to believe. What are some examples of that? How can we "live by believing and not by seeing" when our lives don't match up with what we know we've been promised, yet we continue to wait for?

Meditation moment: Commit to memory at least three of the verses that affirm who God is: that He is true to His Word, that what He says will come to pass, and that He is always working on our behalf. Write them in your journal and seek them out when doubt starts to seep in. Using your journal, commit what you are waiting for within the pages and ask God to show you that He has not forgotten you, and that His promise still stands, because it does!